PRAISE FOR *THE BALANCED MAN*

"This book is a deep and honest introspection of the human condition and our true identity as a species. I highly recommend this book to any man who struggles to find deeper meaning in this world, or anyone who wants to show up better and more stable for everyone around them."

—**Danny Goler,** independent consciousness researcher, founder of Code of Reality Initiative

"In a world of chaos, Terry Bullman's book is an oasis of calm. He shows men how to create the life they want, despite the obstacles of our modern culture. Read this book to learn how to live, love, and celebrate your masculinity and find your true purpose. Five stars. Highly recommended."

—**Dr. Helen Smith,** author of *Men on Strike* and *His Side: Men Speak Out on Marriage, Dating, and Life in America*

"Terry Bullman is the real deal. He's done the work physically, mentally, and spiritually—and it radiates from him. Anything he has to say, I want to listen to closely. This book is a gift."

—**Penny Simon,** VP/Executive Publicist, Crown Publishing Group

"*The Balanced Man* is not a comfortable read—and that's exactly why it matters. Terry challenges men to stop outsourcing their power, confront the war within, and take radical responsibility for who they are becoming. This book doesn't offer surface-level motivation. It offers a mirror—and the courage to look into it."

—**Ethan Wall,** author, speaker, and founder, The Social Media Law Firm

"This book brought a tear to my eyes. If you are looking for powerful Truth, look no further."

—**Jeremy Jackson,** former *Baywatch* star and founder of Inner G Breathwork

THE BALANCED MAN

THE BALANCED MAN

We Are All God.
We Are All the Devil.

Your 30-Day Field Manual for
Winning the War Within

TERRY BULLMAN

Published by Thought Leader Academy Publishing
3901 N Kildare Ave
Chicago, Il 60641

Hardcover ISBN: 978-1-968668-18-1
Paperback ISBN: 978-1-968668-16-7
Ebook ISBN: 978-1-968668-17-4

For Lizzy,
Thank you for walking through the fire with me.

For Trent and Jdub,
*Thanks so much for being part of my
motivation to be a good man, and may you
remember who you are and live like it.*

To God,
*Thank you for the awakening that made
this possible.*

CONTENTS

ACKNOWLEDGMENTS

This book was not written in isolation.

First, to my wife, Lizzy. You've walked with me through every season: the risks, the doubts, the big moves, the growth, and the hard conversations. Moving to Costa Rica wasn't just a change of address. It was a leap of faith. Thank you for believing in the vision, for grounding me when I needed it, and for challenging me to become a better man behind closed doors, not just in public.

To my sons, Trent and Jdub. You are two of the greatest motivations in my life. Watching you grow has pushed me to grow. You don't need a perfect father, but you deserve one who is disciplined, honest, and willing to do the work. This book is part of that commitment.

To the men who have come through our retreats, trained with me, and trusted me with their stories. You sharpen me as much as I challenge you. Your honesty, your struggles, and your breakthroughs have shaped these pages more than you know.

To the mentors, coaches, and friends who called me higher when comfort would have been easier. Thank you for not letting me stay small.

To my parents and family, thank you for the foundation you provided. Work ethic, resilience, and faith were planted early.

And most importantly, to God. For the awakening, the correction, the discipline, and for the grace. Every lesson, every humbling moment, and every breakthrough began there.

This book is a reflection of that journey.

INTRODUCTION

Before we go any further, let me tell you what this book is and what it's not.

This isn't a self-help book full of recycled tips and surface-level advice. I didn't write it to give you a checklist or make you feel good for a few pages. I wrote it because I believe most men are sleepwalking through life, disconnected from who they are and what they're capable of. I've been there myself.

This is a wake-up call. A conversation. An invitation to remember what you already know deep down: that you have more power than you think. That you're not here to live small. That everything you need is already within you.

Each chapter is designed to challenge you, to pull something out of you, and to help you rebuild from the inside out. Some chapters might hit hard. Others might sit with you for days before making sense of it. That's the point.

You don't have to read this cover to cover in one sitting. In fact, I hope you don't. Take your time. Let each chapter settle. Reflect. Journal. Try the daily task at the end if it speaks to you. Let the words do more than sit on a page. Let them move you.

So let's start with an idea that might sound bold. Even a little crazy.

I'M NOT SAYING I'M GOD...
BUT MAYBE I AM

> **"You are gods; you are all sons of the Most High."**
> —Jesus Christ

We Are All God.

I remember the first time I said that out loud.

The words left my mouth, and I could see it instantly in people's faces. Some nodded in understanding, but most looked at me like I had lost my dang mind. Raised eyebrows. Sideways glances. That slight shift in body language said, *"Who does this guy think he is?"*

And I get it. The word "God" is heavy. It carries weight, history, and rules. People hear it and immediately go to the image they were given as children: some bearded figure on a throne, judging, punishing, rewarding.

So when you say *We Are All God*, it sounds like blasphemy. Like arrogance. Like you're putting yourself on a pedestal.

But that's not what I mean at all.

THE MISUNDERSTANDING OF "GOD."

This isn't about ego. It's not about control, or superiority, or thinking you're above anyone else. If anything, it's the opposite.

What I mean is that inside each of us is a piece of something greater. A spark of creation. The same force that made the stars, the oceans, and the mountains. That same force runs through you, through me, through all of us.

Think about it.

We create life. We build, we destroy, we love, we shape the world around us. Every choice we make ripples outward, affecting people, altering futures, shifting realities. That's not just existing. That's power.

And the moment we recognize that, we stop waiting for permission. We stop handing over responsibility for our lives. We stop looking to something outside of ourselves to save us.

Because we realize that we are the ones shaping everything.

THE EGO VS. THE DIVINE

Now, here's where people get it twisted.

The moment you begin to see yourself as connected to something divine, the ego will try to hijack that connection. It'll whisper in your ear, *Yeah, you're God. That means you're special. That means you're better than them. Other people aren't on your level.*

And that's when you've lost the point entirely.

What I believe to be true is that we are all God. Not just me. Not just you. Every single person walking this earth carries the same potential inside them. The only difference is who chooses to wake up to it and who stays asleep.

The ego wants power, control, and recognition. The divine within you? It doesn't need any of that. It just creates. It just is.

So, the real battle isn't about proving whether you're God. It's about remembering that so is everyone else. And if you truly believe that you won't place yourself above anyone, you'll just focus on lifting them.

OWNING POWER WITHOUT LETTING IT OWN YOU

There's a fine line between embracing your power and letting it consume you.

Some people hear *We Are All God* and take it as an excuse to do whatever they want. They see it as a free pass for their ego to run wild.

But if you truly understood what this meant, you'd see that it comes with weight. Responsibility. A real creator doesn't just take, he gives. He serves. He builds something that lasts.

So, if you're walking around acting like you're better than everyone, you've missed it.

True strength isn't about what you can get. It's about what you can give.

True power isn't about being above others. It's about bringing them up with you.

The Bottom Line: You Are the Miracle You've Been Waiting For.

At the end of the day, this isn't about titles, labels, or religious arguments.

It's about a simple truth: You are not powerless.

You are not at the mercy of fate, waiting for some divine intervention to change your life.

You are the intervention.

You are the force that shapes your reality.

The moment you understand that, everything shifts. You stop making excuses. You stop waiting. You stop looking outside yourself for answers and start creating them.

That's what *We Are All God* really means. Not that we are something to be worshiped, but that we are something to be responsible for.

Because whether you create something beautiful or something destructive…

That choice has always been yours.

DAY 1 TASK: CLAIM

Take 10 quiet minutes today. Sit somewhere you won't be interrupted.

Ask yourself:

- Where in my life am I waiting for someone else to save me, fix me, or choose for me?
- What would change if I truly believed I was the one with the power to shift it?

Write down one sentence that starts with:

"If I remembered I am the creator of my life, I would…"

Then finish the sentence. Don't overthink it. Just write.

Say it out loud.

Let your voice carry the weight of your truth.

CHAPTER 2

THE GREAT FORGETTING

REMEMBERING WHO WE ARE

If you're willing to claim that power-not to dominate, but to create-then the next step is learning how to stop giving it away.

In one story, you are the hero. In another, you are the villain.

The truth is, you are both and neither.

Since the beginning of time, humanity has wrestled with the same questions.

Who are we?

Why are we here?

What is the meaning of all of this?

Religions, philosophies, and spiritual traditions have all pointed to the same truth, yet over time, we have forgotten it.

We were born into this world as creators. Not just passive beings experiencing life, but the architects of reality itself.

And yet, something happened.

We were taught to believe we were powerless.

We were told to obey, not to question.

We were made to forget.

And so, we did.

THE TRUTH HAS ALWAYS BEEN KNOWN

This idea isn't new. It has existed across every major religious and spiritual tradition, hidden in ancient texts and passed down through generations.

"So, God created man in His own image." (Genesis 1:27)

"The kingdom of God is within you." (Luke 17:21)

If we were created in the image of God, then what does that make us?

If God is within us, then why have we spent our lives searching for Him outside of ourselves?

Hinduism teaches that we are all fragments of Brahman, the ultimate reality, divine sparks who have forgotten their true nature.

Taoism speaks of Yin and Yang, the eternal balance of creation and destruction, both of which exist inside of us.

Kabbalah describes the human soul as a piece of God, hidden in the physical world, waiting to be remembered.

Every tradition has known the truth.

But we were taught something else.

We were told to fear.

We were told that questioning was dangerous.

We were told that we were small, limited, and at the mercy of forces beyond our control.

And so, we became prisoners of our own forgetting.

RAISED IN THE FEAR OF QUESTIONING

I was raised to believe in absolutes.

Good and evil.

Right and wrong.

Heaven and hell.

My father, Red Bullman, was a Baptist preacher. His sermons were filled with fire and brimstone, his voice shaking the church walls, making grown men tremble.

And growing up in the Reagan Era, there was no gray area.

Drugs? Evil.

Rock music? Evil.

Anything that made you question authority? Dangerous.

I was taught that every action had eternal consequences.

Do the right thing, and you go to Heaven.

Make the wrong choice, and you burn in Hell.

There was no room for questioning. No space for doubt.

You obeyed. Or you suffered.

And for a long time, I never questioned it.

Until Costa Rica. Until the mountain. Until the moment that shattered everything, I thought I knew.

THE AWAKENING ON THE MOUNTAIN

I had been invited to a plant medicine ceremony.

Per usual, even though I had zero experience with any kinds of drugs or plant medicines, really, I went all in and consumed seven grams of psilocybin. What's known as a heroic dose.

I don't know what compelled me to say yes. Maybe it was the energy of Costa Rica, or maybe it was something deeper, a pull toward a truth I had always known but never dared to face.

I lay down, staring at the wooden beams of the Shala. The setting sun cast golden light through a triangular cutout in the roof framing.

And suddenly, I was the newborn Christ in the manger.

Not in a religious sense, but in an existential one.

I felt myself being born again-not into a new faith, but into a truth that had always been inside me.

Then my friend, the one who had invited me, walked by.

He was wearing all white, with a massive beard.

In my altered state, I looked up at him and asked, "Jesus?"

He smiled and said, "Nope, not even close."

But the message had already been delivered.

God wasn't outside of me.

God was inside of me.

And I had always been carrying Him.

VISIONS OF TRUTH

I saw sacred geometry, pyramids, and Africa.

At one point, I even saw myself as a gorilla-something ancient, something primal, something I couldn't yet put into words.

And then, my eyes locked onto the wooden beams of the Shala, following them upward until I reached the Wi-Fi antenna mounted on the roof.

I was furious.

Technology was poisoning the world.

It was pulling us away from nature, from spirit, from truth.

It was keeping us asleep.

But then the realization hit me.

Technology is neither good nor evil. It is a tool.

Like fire. Like the written word. Like anything else, it depends on how we use it.

Just like us.

We can be God, or we can be the Devil.

It is always a choice.

That day, my mind cracked open.

That day, I started to remember.

> **"You are not a drop in the ocean. You are the entire ocean in a drop."**
> —Rumi

THE GREAT REMEMBERING

We have been told a lie.

We have been told that we are separate from God.

We have been told that we are at the mercy of fate.

We have been told that we are powerless to change our lives.

But ancient wisdom, across religions, philosophies, and every spiritual tradition has always said otherwise.

God is within you.

You are creating your reality in every moment.

You are both the light and the darkness, the architect of your own heaven or hell.

The Devil is not some red-skinned beast lurking in the shadows.

The Devil is forgetting.

Forgetting who you are.

Forgetting your power.

Forgetting that you always could create or destroy.

And that means…

The Devil wins when we let the world tell us that we are powerless.

The Devil wins when we let fear keep us asleep.

The Devil wins when we stop questioning, stop seeking, stop creating.

But here's the thing.

The moment we remember, the spell is broken.

The moment we wake up, the game changes.

The moment we reclaim our power, the Devil loses.

THE CHOICE HAS ALWAYS BEEN YOURS

You are both God and the Devil.

The only question is, which one will you listen to?

Because whether you realize it or not, you have always had the power to choose.

And now that you've begun to remember, the next question is,

What are you going to do with it?

DAY 2 TASK: REMEMBER

Today, set aside 15 minutes to reflect on your story.

Ask yourself:

- Where in my life have I forgotten who I am?
- What beliefs, fears, or systems have convinced me I'm small or powerless?

Write down three ways you've handed over your power in the past.

Then write one bold sentence that begins with:

"I am no longer afraid to…"

Speak it.

Claim it.

And remember, this is you, waking up.

CHAPTER 3

THE BATTLE WITHIN

FEAR, POWER, AND THE WAR FOR YOUR SOUL

Now that you've begun to remember, the next question is, what are you going to do with it?

There's a moment that comes after every great awakening- a moment where you realize that just because you've seen the truth doesn't mean you've become it.

I had just come down from the most intense spiritual experience of my life. I had seen visions, felt an undeniable connection to something greater, and broken free, at least, that's what I thought. But in the days that followed, something darker crept in.

Doubt. Resistance. Fear.

The high of the revelation faded, and in its place, the old voices returned.

What if it was all just a hallucination?

What if I've lost my mind?

What if I've strayed too far from the faith I was raised in?

And that's when I realized: awakening is just the first battle.

The real war is learning how to live with it.

THE GOD VS. DEVIL BATTLE INSIDE YOU

Most people spend their whole lives fearing the Devil. They imagine him as some external force, lurking in the shadows, waiting to strike.

But what if he isn't out there at all?

What if the Devil is the voice in your head telling you you're not good enough, not smart enough, not strong enough?

What if he's been with you this whole time?

And what if God has, too?

For centuries, we've been told that God and the Devil are at war. Good versus evil. Light versus darkness. Heaven versus Hell.

But what if this war isn't happening outside of you?

What if it's happening inside your own mind?

Every day, in every moment, you are choosing which force to align with.

The real battlefield isn't in some unseen spiritual realm; it's within your own thoughts, your own decisions, your own ability to rise or fall.

God and the Devil are not somewhere out there.

They are both inside of you.

> **"The mind is its own place, and in itself can make
> a heaven of hell, a hell of heaven."**
> —John Milton

THE TWO WOLVES INSIDE YOU

Religions and philosophies have always pointed to this inner struggle.

Paul, in his letters to the Romans, described it perfectly:

> *"For I do not do the good I want to do, but the evil I do not
> want to do, this I keep on doing."*

He was wrestling with the same battle we all face: the pull between light and darkness inside us.

The book of James puts it another way:

> *"Each person is tempted when they are dragged away by their
> own evil desire and enticed."*

Temptation doesn't come from the outside. It doesn't show up in a red cape with horns and a pitchfork. It comes from within.

The Cherokee tell the story of the two wolves. An elder explains to his grandson, "Inside every person, there are two wolves. One is evil - anger, greed, envy, fear. The other is good- love, peace, courage, kindness."

The grandson asks, "Which wolf wins?"

The elder replies, "The one you feed."

Taoism teaches that light and dark are not enemies. They are part of the same whole. Balance is key.

Which means the goal is not to kill the Devil inside you, it's to learn how to master him.

THE BATTLE BETWEEN YOUR HEART AND MIND

I've come to realize something.

Your heart represents God.

Your mind represents the Devil.

Your heart knows what is true. It speaks in love, courage, and faith.

Your mind creates fear, doubt, and self-sabotage.

The mind's job is to keep you safe, which often means keeping you small. It whispers, *"Stay comfortable."*

The heart whispers, *leap*.

The challenge is learning which voice to listen to.

FEAR AS A PRISON, THE ILLUSION OF SAFETY

I see it in men all the time.

The fear of leaving the job they hate.

The fear of walking away from a relationship that's draining them.

The fear of pursuing something bigger because they might fail.

So, they stay locked in their own personal hell, convincing themselves that it's safer inside.

But the bars of their prison aren't real.

I know because I lived there.

For years, I let fear run my life. I played it safe; I followed the rules, I stayed in my lane because that's what I was taught.

But what if I told you that fear is just a test?

That it's the doorway to your next level?

That fear isn't there to stop you; it's there to see if you're ready.

MASTERING FEAR-TURNING THE DEVIL INTO YOUR ALLY

There are two ways to deal with fear. You can let it keep you where you are, or you can use it as fuel.

The difference between those who create and those who stay stuck isn't that they don't feel fear; it's that they act anyway.

Because courage isn't the absence of fear.

Courage is looking fear in the eye and saying, "Not today, devil."

Courage is using fear as a guide, not a roadblock.

Because here's what I believe:

The thing you're most afraid of is usually the very thing you're meant to do.

If you weren't meant for more, you wouldn't feel that pull.

If you weren't supposed to step into something greater, you wouldn't feel resistance.

Your fear is proof that something bigger is waiting for you.

The question is, will you let it stop you?

Or will you step through it and claim what's yours?

WINNING THE BATTLE INSIDE YOU

The war inside you will never fully end. But you can learn to control which voice you listen to.

First, identify the two voices.

When doubt creeps in, ask yourself: *Who is speaking?*

Is this fear talking? Or faith?

Is this self-sabotage? Or self-belief?

Second, starve the Devil, feed the God.

The Devil thrives on fear, laziness, and weakness.

The God force grows with discipline, action, and faith.

Every decision you make strengthens one or the other.

Third, control your thoughts.

Your mind will try to trick you into staying where you are.

When negative thoughts creep in, don't believe them.

You are not your thoughts. You are the observer of them.

You don't have to let the Devil run your life.

But you do have to recognize when he's speaking.

THE TRUTH YOU MUST REMEMBER

You are not powerless in this battle.

The Devil is not outside of you; he's in your mind.

But so is God.

Every day, every moment, you are choosing who to listen to.

The life you build will depend on which voice you follow.

Master the battle inside, and you master life itself.

And once you've learned to listen, really listen, to the voice that lifts you, you're ready to begin building a life that reflects it.

DAY 3 TASK: FACE THE VOICE

Take 10 minutes today to sit quietly and listen.

Ask yourself:

- What voice is the loudest in my life right now - fear or faith?
- What is one decision I've been avoiding because of fear?

Now write down two columns:

- **Column 1:** What the fear voice is saying
- **Column 2:** What your higher self, your God voice, knows to be true

Choose one action today that aligns with the God voice.

Something small, but bold.

You feed the voice you listen to.

Make sure it's the one that leads you forward.

CHAPTER 4

THE MANY NAMES OF GOD

Once you learn to master the battle within, you're no longer just surviving; you're ready to seek something deeper. Something greater. The source behind the voice you've chosen to follow.

I remember sitting in church as a kid, listening to my father preach about the one true God. The message was clear- there was one path, one truth, one way. Anything outside of that was dangerous, even evil.

And I believed it.

Until life made me question everything.

I've sat with shamans in the jungle, watching them call upon spirits older than any book I'd ever read. I've spoken to Buddhists who described enlightenment in ways that felt eerily like the "salvation" I had been taught. I've read ancient Hindu texts that describe the divine not as some distant being but as something within me, within all of us.

And I started to wonder:

If all these different people, in different parts of the world, across thousands of years, were all reaching for the same thing…

Could they really all be wrong?

Or had we just been given different pieces of the same puzzle?

ONE STORY, MANY TRANSLATIONS

The more I studied, the more I saw the threads that connected all religions. It was like seeing the same story told in different languages, each one shaped by the culture and time in which it was written.

They all spoke of light and darkness.

Of God and the Devil.

Of struggle, redemption, and the path to becoming whole.

Jesus spoke of salvation and love.

Buddha spoke of enlightenment and compassion.

Krishna spoke of dharma and self-realization.

Different words. Same meaning.

Even the idea of heaven and hell existed everywhere, but not always as literal places. In some traditions, they were states of mind, consequences of how we chose to live. Some saw them as realms, others as energy. But the message was always the same- our actions, our choices, our hearts determined where we existed.

Could the truth be too big for just one religion to hold?

> **"The lamps are different, but the Light is the same."**
> —Rumi

THE MOUNTAIN OF GOD

I once heard a metaphor that stuck with me.

Imagine God as a mountain, and humanity standing at the base, trying to reach the summit.

Some take one path. Others take another. Some paths are straight and steep, others are winding and slow. Some travelers use ropes and tools, while others climb with nothing but their hands.

From the ground, it looks like everyone is going a different way.

Some yell across the mountain, insisting that their path is the only one that leads to the top.

Others scoff at different travelers, certain they're lost.

But from above, from the summit, something different is revealed.

All the paths lead to the same place.

Some just take longer than others.

What if that's what religion is?

What if every sacred text, every tradition, every practice is just a different route up the same mountain?

RELIGION VS. SPIRITUALITY— THE SHIFT IN THINKING

For years, I wrestled with the difference between religion and spirituality.

I had been taught that spirituality without structure was dangerous, that without rules, without doctrine, you'd be lost.

But then I saw something else.

Religions are institutions. They have hierarchies, rules, and politics. And like all human institutions, they can be corrupted. They can be used to control, to separate, to instill fear. Wars have been fought over whose version of God is the "right" one.

But spirituality? That's personal. That's the direct connection. It's the raw experience of the divine, without a middleman.

I started meeting more people who didn't fit into a religious box but were deeply spiritual. People who didn't go to church but lived by principles of love, compassion, and service. People who didn't pray in the traditional sense but who meditated, connected with nature, and sought wisdom in their own ways.

And I realized something:

Maybe God isn't in the building.

Maybe He's in the space between us.

Maybe He's in the wind, in the ocean, in the breath we take when we're fully present.

Maybe the search for God isn't about choosing the right religion.

Maybe it's about remembering that He's never been separate from us to begin with.

THE CORRUPTION OF TRUTH

It's not the teachings that divide us. It's the people who twist them.

There's nothing wrong with Christianity, Islam, Buddhism, or any other faith at their core.

The problem isn't in the message; it's in how people have used them.

How many wars have been fought in the name of religion?

How many people have been condemned, shamed, or killed over differences in belief?

How many institutions have hoarded wealth while preaching about humility?

And yet, Jesus wasn't a man of riches.

Buddha gave up a kingdom to seek enlightenment.

The prophets lived humbly, serving others rather than themselves.

The real enemy isn't religion.

It's those who use it to control rather than uplift.

Because God isn't a set of rules.

God isn't a brand.

God is love.

And anything that moves us toward love moves us toward Him.

THE ONE TRUTH THAT CONNECTS US ALL

If we strip away the labels, the rituals, the doctrines, what's left?

Every tradition, at its highest level, teaches the same truth:

We are all connected.

We are here to grow.

We are here to love.

We are here to become whole.

Call it Christ-consciousness.

Call it enlightenment.

Call it divine energy.

Call it whatever you want.

But when you get rid of the walls, we are all searching for the same thing.

And when we realize that, the divisions disappear.

Because at the summit of the mountain, there is no separation.

Just one truth, shining down on all of us.

FINAL THOUGHT: THE LANGUAGE OF GOD

If there's one thing I've learned, it's this: God speaks in many languages.

Sometimes He speaks through scripture.

Sometimes He speaks through silence.

Sometimes He speaks through the people we meet, the struggles we face, and the beauty we witness.

And sometimes, if we're really listening, He speaks through all of them at once.

And when we begin to hear that voice in our own lives, not just through books or buildings, but in breath, in pain, in connection, we realize the journey isn't just about reaching the top of the mountain.

It's about walking each step in truth.

DAY 4 TASK: RECLAIM THE DIVINE

Today, reflect on your own spiritual upbringing.

Ask yourself:

- What beliefs about God or spirituality did I inherit from others?
- Which of those beliefs still feel true in my body, and which ones feel like fear or guilt?

Then, complete this sentence in your journal:

"For me, God feels like…"

Write without judgment. Without rules.

Not what you were told—what you feel.

This is your first step in building a direct relationship with the divine, on your own terms.

CHAPTER 5

FAITH, FEAR, AND THE FINE LINE BETWEEN SEEKING AND STRAYING

Once you begin to hear God in everything, not just in scriptures but in silence, in struggle, in beauty, you can't unhear it. But that doesn't mean the old voices go silent. Sometimes, they get louder.

I can still hear my father's voice, deep and certain, preaching from the pulpit of that small Baptist church. The rhythm of his words, the conviction in his tone, the way the congregation responded with *amens* and *hallelujahs*, it was all so ingrained in me, it felt like a part of my DNA.

There were things I knew without question. God was good. The Devil was real. The world was dangerous, full of temptations designed to pull you away from the truth.

And now, years later, after everything I'd seen, everything I'd learned, everything I had dared to question, I still carried that voice with me.

Maybe that's why, despite all my growth, I still wrestled with the thought:

Am I being deceived?

Because if my father were still alive, and if I told him that plant medicine had given me some of the clearest spiritual revelations of my life, that I was writing a book questioning traditional interpretations of faith, that I was exploring truths beyond the walls of the church, what would he say?

Would he see me as lost? As someone who had strayed too far? Would he pray for me to come back to the light, believing that the world had swallowed me up?

That thought haunted me.

Because what if he was right?

> **"Doubt is not the opposite of faith;**
> **it is one element of faith."**
> —Paul Tillich

THE FEAR OF QUESTIONING FAITH

When you're raised in the church, faith isn't just a belief, it's an identity. And when you start to challenge certain teachings, it doesn't just feel like you're questioning ideas. It feels like you're tearing away a piece of yourself.

I was taught that there was one path to God and stepping outside of that path was dangerous. Seeking wisdom from anything outside of scripture could open doors to deception. The world was full of traps, designed to pull you away from faith.

But the more I lived, the more I saw the cracks in that way of thinking.

Because wasn't Jesus Himself a challenger of the religious system? Didn't He reject rigid doctrine in favor of direct connection to God?

Maybe questioning wasn't a sign of weakness.

It could be the path to a deeper, more unshakable faith.

I had to ask myself:

Was my fear of *being deceived* really about God?

Or was it about the conditioning I had received as a child?

Was I afraid of losing my faith?

Or was I afraid of outgrowing the version of faith I had been given?

PLANT MEDICINE: DARKNESS OR CLARITY?

I won't lie: the first time I sat in a plant medicine ceremony, a small part of me was waiting for some great punishment to befall me.

Would I feel darkness creeping in? Would I sense that I had opened myself up to something evil?

But what I experienced was the opposite.

I felt layers of fear, conditioning, and self-imposed limitations peeling away. I saw my own patterns, where I was holding myself back, where I was clinging to old wounds. And underneath it all, I felt something I hadn't expected.

God.

Not in the way I had been taught, not as a distant figure sitting on a throne, watching, and judging. But as something alive, something present, something woven into the very fabric of my being.

The experience didn't pull me away from God.

It brought me closer.

So why did I still feel guilty?

Because I had been taught that any path outside of scripture was dangerous.

And yet, if God created all things, if He designed the very plants of the earth, then why would He not also create ways for us to see Him more clearly?

The Bible warns against being deceived, but it also says, *"You will seek me and find me when you seek me with all your heart."*

And wasn't that what I was doing?

Seeking?

THE FEAR OF BEING SWALLOWED BY THE WORLD

There's a difference between questioning faith and abandoning it.

The Bible warns against being consumed by the world, but what does that really mean?

Does it mean questioning religious institutions?

No. Jesus did that Himself.

Does it mean seeking a deeper understanding beyond what you were taught as a child?

No. Growth requires exploration.

What it does warn against is losing yourself to greed, to power, to materialism, to the endless pursuit of things that don't matter.

And that wasn't what I was doing.

I wasn't chasing money.

I wasn't seeking status.

I wasn't trying to build a kingdom of my own.

I was trying to strip away illusions.

I was trying to find the truth.

I was trying to connect with God in the most real way possible.

And if I had to step outside of traditional teachings to do that, then maybe that wasn't a betrayal of my faith.

It could be the fulfillment of it.

WALKING THE FINE LINE—STAYING GROUNDED WHILE SEEKING

The key wasn't blind faith.

The key wasn't reckless exploration.

The key was balance.

If I were going to walk this path, I had to stay grounded.

I had to ask myself, *does this align with love, with truth, with integrity?*

I had to trust my inner guidance, not fear-based teachings designed to keep people in line.

And most of all, I had to remember that faith and curiosity are not enemies.

Faith isn't about shutting doors to other perspectives.

It's about being so rooted in truth that you don't have to fear exploration.

Because if God is real, truly real, then no amount of questioning will make Him disappear.

FINAL THOUGHTS: GOD IS BIGGER THAN OUR FEARS

At the end of the day, I had to come to peace with one thing:

God is bigger than any single religion.

Bigger than any church.

Bigger than any rulebook.

If my search were genuine, if my heart was truly seeking Him, then He would meet me wherever I was.

In prayer.

In silence.

In scripture.

In plant medicine.

In nature.

In life itself.

God isn't afraid of my questions.

My exploration doesn't threaten him.

He made me this way: curious, seeking, unwilling to accept shallow answers.

And maybe, just maybe, the greatest act of faith isn't blind obedience.

It's trusting that your path to God doesn't have to look like anyone else's.

Because the voice of truth doesn't just echo in a sanctuary.

It speaks in the silence you sit with.

It shows up in the questions you dare to ask.

And if you can trust that voice, your own knowing, you're ready for what comes next.

DAY 5 TASK: TRUST YOUR SEEKER

Write down three beliefs you were raised with about God or spirituality that you've begun to question.

Now ask yourself:

- Am I questioning this because I'm being rebellious?
- Or because something deeper is calling me to explore?

Then, finish this sentence in your journal:

"If I believed God was not afraid of my questions, I would…"

Let that answer guide your next step.

Don't run from the questions. Walk with them.

This is what real faith looks like.

CHAPTER 6

HEAVEN AND HELL

JUST ONE DECISION AWAY

If God is bigger than your fears, then so are you. But stepping into that truth requires something most of us avoid: choosing differently when everything in you wants to stay the same.

I used to think heaven and hell were places, somewhere we either earned our way into or got condemned to. I was raised to believe that every action, every choice, was stacking up points in one column or the other, like some divine scoreboard tallying up my fate.

But the more I lived, the more I realized something…

Heaven and hell aren't places we go after we die.

They're right here. Right now.

I've stood in a room filled with everything I thought I wanted: money, success, respect, and felt like I was suffocating in hell. And I've sat in absolute silence, on a mountain in Costa Rica, with nothing but my breath and the sound of the ocean in the distance, and felt like I was touching heaven.

It's not about what you have, where you are, or even what happens to you.

It's about how you respond.

It's about the decisions you make, one after the other.

And the space between heaven and hell?

It's thinner than we think.

THE ILLUSION OF DISTANCE

People talk about heaven like it's some place in the clouds, full of angels and golden gates.

They talk about hell like it's some fiery pit beneath the earth, waiting to swallow up sinners.

But I've seen men living in hell while sitting in million-dollar mansions.

I've seen people with nothing walk around in a state of peace that no amount of money could buy.

The truth is, heaven and hell aren't distant realms.

They exist in the same space, stacked on top of each other, coexisting in every moment.

And we slip between them more than we realize.

One moment, you're at peace: grateful, connected, full of life.

One thought, one decision, and suddenly, you're somewhere else.

Trapped in regret.

Consumed by anger.

Overcome by fear.

It doesn't take much to fall from heaven.

And it doesn't take much to climb out of hell, either.

ONE DECISION CAN CHANGE EVERYTHING

There's a moment in every man's life where one decision takes him somewhere he never thought he'd go.

Maybe it's the decision to walk away from an argument instead of throwing a punch.

Maybe it's choosing to swallow your pride and apologize instead of doubling down on your ego.

Maybe it's the decision to stay when it would've been easier to leave.

I've had those moments.

I've also had the opposite.

I've made one wrong move, said one wrong thing, let anger, fear, or pride steer me for just a second, and ended up in a hell of my own making.

The older I get, the more I realize that life isn't just one big battle between good and evil; it's a thousand small ones.

And every choice, no matter how small, is leading you closer to one or the other.

It's never just about the moment.

It's about what that moment leads to.

> "Between stimulus and response, there is a space.
> In that space is our power to choose our response.
> In our response lies our growth and our freedom."
> —Viktor Frankl

WHEN MY WORLD BURNED DOWN

I've lived through my own version of hell.

When COVID hit, it wasn't just a health crisis; it was a warzone for small business owners.

The gyms I had poured my life into, the places I had built from the ground up, were suddenly bleeding money.

Lockdowns. Restrictions. People are afraid to train.

I fought it for as long as I could. I threw everything I had at keeping them alive, but the numbers didn't lie.

I lost them.

Filing for bankruptcy was one of the hardest things I've ever done.

The gym wasn't just a business; it was a piece of me.

It was my identity, my legacy, my blood and sweat poured into brick and mortar.

And just like that, it was gone.

And for a while, so was I.

I fell into the darkest hole I had ever known.

It wasn't just financial. It was emotional, mental, and spiritual.

I questioned everything: who I was without those gyms, what the point of all my work had been, and whether I had failed not just myself but the people who had put their trust in me. That was hell.

> **"No man ever steps in the same river twice, for it's not the same river and he's not the same man."**
> —Heraclitus

THE REBIRTH

But then, something shifted.

One day, after spending weeks drowning in anger, regret, and shame, I realized something:

I was still here.

And, as long as I was still breathing, I had a choice.

I could keep replaying my loss, keep feeding the fire of my own destruction, or I could start climbing.

One decision.

One moment.

One shift in perspective.

And here's the thing, I thought losing my gyms was the end.

But it was the beginning.

Letting go of those gyms freed me.

It allowed me to step fully into the life I was meant to live.

It gave me the space, energy, and clarity to pour myself into my retreat center in Nosara, a place where I could impact men on a deeper level than I ever could within four walls.

The thing that I thought was my destruction was my rebirth.

Hell only lasted as long as I refused to let go.

Once I did, I found myself in heaven.

And it all came down to one decision.

The question is, what decision are you sitting in right now? And what would change if you made a different one?

DAY 6 TASK: CHOOSE YOUR EXIT

Think about a situation in your life right now that feels like a personal hell, big or small.

Ask yourself:

- What decision am I making (or avoiding) that's keeping me here?
- What's the one next right action that would move me even one step closer to peace?

Then write this sentence in your journal and finish it:

"Heaven is on the other side of…"

Let your next action move you in that direction.

Hell ends the moment you decide it does.

CHAPTER 7

THE ILLUSION OF GOOD AND EVIL

HOW THE MODERN WORLD MANIPULATES MEN

Heaven and hell aren't places. They're choices. But when the world sells you a lie about what it means to be a man, even the wrong choices can feel like survival.

Since the beginning of time, men have been taught to see the world in black and white: good versus evil, right versus wrong, strength versus weakness. This duality is comforting because it makes life seem simple. It gives us heroes to admire and villains to blame.

But the truth is, reality isn't that clear-cut.

And in today's world, the illusion of duality is being weaponized against men.

It's used to divide us.

To control us.

To distract us from what truly matters.

We're told:

- If you're not winning, you're losing.
- If you're not at the top, you're failing.
- If you don't have money, power, or status, you're weak.

And because men are wired to seek purpose and achievement, many fall for this trap.

They buy into the influencer lifestyle, the grind culture, the idea that they need to dominate to be respected.

But what if this entire system was designed to keep men lost, chasing validation instead of meaning?

What if the real battle isn't between good and evil *out there* but inside our own minds?

THE WEAPONIZATION OF DUALITY— A SYSTEM BUILT TO DIVIDE

The more divided men are, the easier they are to control.

Society does this by keeping us stuck in false choices:

- **Alpha or Beta**—You're either a dominant, powerful leader or a weak, submissive follower. No room for balance, wisdom, or individuality.
- **Winner or Loser**—Your worth is determined by how much money you make, how many women you attract, and how many people look up to you.
- **Ruler or Enslaved**—Either you exploit the system for your own gain, or you get crushed by it.

And what happens when men believe in these extremes?

- They chase money at the expense of purpose.
- They become addicted to status, rather than fulfillment.
- They turn against each other instead of uniting.

Look at the influencer economy, so-called "men's coaches" who start out wanting to help but get sucked into the ego trap.

They flash their wealth, their cars, their watches, making other men feel small so that they'll pay to learn "the secret."

But here's what they aren't telling you: There is no secret.

They're just selling the illusion.

They're playing the same game they claim to be exposing.

And the more men who fall for it, the more this cycle continues.

This isn't a strength.

It's insecurity masked as power.

THE BATTLE BETWEEN THE MIND AND THE HEART

If we are both God and the Devil, then the real war is inside of us.

The **mind** is where fear, doubt, and ego live.

It tells you:

- "You're not enough."
- "You need more to be valuable."
- "You must prove your worth to the world."

The **heart** is where wisdom, courage, and truth live.

It reminds you:

- "You already have everything you need."
- "True power isn't about control, it's about mastery."
- "You are here to serve, not just to take."

The problem is that modern society rewards the mind and ignores the heart.

It glorifies external success but ridicules emotional intelligence.

It tells men to dominate instead of lead.

To accumulate instead of creating.

But real men, *balanced* men, know that true strength isn't about how much you can take.

It's about how much you can give.

> **"Knowing others is intelligence; knowing yourself is true wisdom."**
> —Lao Tzu

BREAKING FREE—HOW TO RISE ABOVE THE ILLUSION

If the system is built to keep men distracted, how do we break free?

1. Redefine Success

Success isn't just about money or status. It's about *alignment*, living with integrity, building something meaningful, and leaving a real impact.

Ask yourself:

If I had everything society says I should want, would I feel fulfilled?

2. Stop Seeking External Validation

If you're chasing wealth, women, or admiration just to feel "worthy," you're a slave to the system.

True confidence comes from self-mastery, not from applause.

3. Master the Ego Before It Masters You

Ego isn't bad, it's just a tool.

But left unchecked, it will destroy everything you're trying to build.

The moment success becomes about proving yourself to others instead of fulfilling your mission, you've already lost.

4. Find Strength in Balance

Society tells you that men must either be cold, dominant, and emotionless or soft, weak, and passive.

The truth?

The strongest men are both warriors and nurturers.

They know when to be hard and when to be soft.

They lead with both discipline and compassion.

FINAL THOUGHT: CHOOSING THE PATH OF THE WISE WARRIOR

The foolish man chases money, power, and status, thinking it will bring him peace.

He becomes trapped in his own ego, always needing more, never satisfied.

The wise warrior seeks balance.

He is strong, but compassionate.

Focused, but flexible.

He builds wealth without compromising his integrity.

He earns respect but doesn't need it to validate his worth.

The world is full of men being led astray, taught to measure their value in numbers rather than by character.

You don't have to be one of them.

The choice is yours:

- Follow the illusion and spend your life chasing things that will never fulfill you.
- Or break free, master yourself, and become a man of true power, wisdom, and purpose.

Because once you stop chasing someone else's idea of success, you create space for something far more powerful:

Your own.

DAY 7 TASK: REDEFINE WHAT MAKES A MAN

Today, take 15 minutes to reflect on what you've been taught about manhood.

Write down:

- Three beliefs you were raised with about what it means to be a "real man."
- Three experiences where those beliefs left you feeling disconnected, insecure, or unfulfilled.

Now ask yourself:

> **What does *my* version of masculinity look like? What kind of man do I want to be?**

End with this sentence:

> **"A powerful man is someone who..."**

Write it. Claim it. Live it.

CHAPTER 8

THE MIRROR EFFECT

WE ARE ALL EACH OTHER'S TEACHERS

The moment you say no to the impulse, no to the escape, no to the lie, you step into something deeper. And that's where the mirror appears. Because now it's not just about you anymore. Now it's about the example you leave behind.

There's a shift that happens in a man's life, though not all men recognize it.

Some feel it creeping in quietly, the moment they realize they're no longer the young warrior, no longer the one charging ahead without question.

Others resist it, clinging to the fire of their youth, trying to outrun time.

But time catches up with all of us.

The real question is: **Do we evolve with it, or do we fight against it?**

For me, this realization came in the gym.

I've spent years teaching young fighters, sharpening their skills, pushing them to be better.

And yet, there are moments when I catch myself slipping into competition mode, when the instinct to dominate still rises in my chest.

The young guys come in hungry, full of energy, eager to test themselves against me.

And I must ask myself, how hard am I supposed to fight back?

There's a fine line between teaching and competing, between guiding and proving something to yourself.

I see this same battle everywhere, not just in fighting.

Men chasing youth through testosterone and reckless competition.

Women filling their faces with Botox and lip fillers, trying to hold onto an image of themselves that time is pulling away from.

No one wants to feel like they're being left behind. No one wants to admit that their role in the story is changing.

But maybe the shift isn't about losing power.

Maybe it's about stepping into a different kind of power altogether.

THE IDENTITY CRISIS: HOLDING ON
VS. LETTING GO

For years, my identity was wrapped up in being a fighter.

Not just in the ring, but in everything I did.

That mentality, the relentless drive, the refusal to quit, the belief that you always have to be the toughest one in the room, became the foundation of who I was.

So, what happens when you're no longer the fastest, strongest, or most dangerous guy in the gym?

For some, the answer is denial. They fight harder. Push further.

Try to stay on top for as long as they can.

They refuse to step aside because stepping aside feels like becoming irrelevant.

But the reality is, **refusing to let go isn't strength, it's fear disguised as strength.**

A real warrior knows when to evolve.

That doesn't mean becoming weak.

It doesn't mean fading into the background.

It means recognizing that wisdom is now your greatest weapon, not brute force.

It means embracing the role of the teacher, the guide, not because you're giving up, but because you've outgrown the need to prove yourself.

THE EGO TRAP: COMPETING VS. LEADING

There's a moment in every warrior's journey when he must decide:

Am I still fighting to win, or am I fighting to teach?

Ego is tricky.

It whispers, *you've still got it. Show them. Make them respect you.*

But true respect isn't earned by beating someone down.

It's earned by lifting someone else.

I think about those younger fighters.

They watch everything.

They see how I handle victories, but more importantly, how I handle the moments when I could choose dominance and instead choose discipline.

Am I going to be the guy who clings to his status?

Or the guy who helps the next generation rise?

This isn't just a lesson for fighters.

It's for the businessman who refuses to mentor younger guys because he still wants to be the top dog.

It's for the father who can't accept that his son is now a man.

It's for anyone who's ever looked in the mirror and asked, *Am I being left behind?*

I believe that you only get left behind if you refuse to move forward.

REDEFINING STRENGTH: WISDOM OVER YOUTH

Society glorifies youth.

It makes people believe that relevance is tied to how fast you move, how hard you hit, and how young you look.

But that's an illusion.

Real relevance isn't about keeping up with the young guys.

It's about having something they *don't* have yet.

Perspective. Experience. Mastery.

It's about knowing when to push, when to step back, and when to let someone else take the lead, not out of weakness, but out of wisdom.

There's a saying: *The best leaders create more leaders, not more followers.*

That's the shift.

The young warrior fights for himself.

The evolved warrior fights for something greater.

> **"What we do for ourselves dies with us. What we do for others and the world remains and is immortal."**
> —Albert Pike

KNOWING WHEN TO CROSS OVER

There's a natural point when every warrior becomes the teacher.

It doesn't happen all at once, but the signs are there if you're paying attention.

For me, it was in the gym, watching a younger fighter make the same reckless mistakes I used to make.

I could've torn through him, shown him the gap between his experience and mine.

But instead, I stopped him mid-round.

I pointed out what he was doing wrong, how he was leaving himself open.

I gave him knowledge instead of bruises.

And I watched as his eyes shifted from frustration to understanding.

That moment?

That was real power.

Not proving myself.

Not holding onto something that was already evolving.

But seeing the impact of passing down what I had learned.

The same is true in life.

There comes a time when competing with youth is pointless because your purpose has changed.

You're no longer in the phase where your value is measured by how hard you hit.

You're in the phase where your value is measured by how much you *give back*.

The question is, are you ready to step into that?

Or are you still trying to outrun time?

FINAL THOUGHT: LEGACY OVER EGO

At some point, you must ask yourself:

What am I really fighting for?

To prove I've still got it?

To compete with younger men?

To hold onto a version of myself that no longer fits?

Or is it something more?

Because time wins. Always.

The men who try to fight it end up bitter, broken, or chasing a crown that no longer matters.

But the men who embrace it?

They become something greater than they ever were in their youth.

They become leaders.

Mentors.

Masters of their craft.

And the impact they leave lasts long after they're gone.

You don't lose your strength by evolving.

You amplify it.

The greatest warriors don't just fight battles.

They create legacies.

And that's the real test, not whether you can still throw the hardest punch,

But whether you can pass down something that will outlive you.

That's what makes a man truly undefeated.

DAY 8 TASK: CHOOSE LEGACY OVER EGO

Today, reflect on this:

- Where in your life are you still competing when you should be leading?
- Where is your ego keeping you in a role you've already outgrown?
- Who around you could grow if you chose to guide instead of proving?

Write this sentence in your journal and complete it:

"The most powerful thing I can pass down is…"

Then take one action today, however small, that reflects that answer.

CHAPTER 9

THE ILLUSION OF FREEDOM

REDEFINING WHAT'S 'OKAY'

Once you stop chasing validation and begin defining your own worth, you'll start to notice just how many distractions you've been using to avoid yourself.

I remember a time when a close friend of mine betrayed someone he loved.

He had been in a long-term relationship, a solid one, or so I thought.

Then one day, over drinks, he admitted he had been cheating. He said it like it was nothing, like it just happened, like it wasn't his fault.

"She doesn't give me what I need," he justified. "I still love her, but man… sometimes you just slip."

I wanted to tell him what a fool he was. I wanted to shake him, to make him see what he was doing.

But I didn't.

Because I had to sit with the uncomfortable truth that I had been on both sides of that kind of pain.

I had been cheated on before. I knew that gut-punch feeling of betrayal, of questioning everything, of wondering what was real.

But I also knew what it was like to be the one making excuses.

I've only ever cheated on one person in my life. And when it happened, the weight of it crushed me.

I told her less than an hour later because I couldn't carry the lie.

But I had also been the "other guy" a few times, willingly stepping into situations I had no business being in, telling myself that if she was cheating, it wasn't on me.

No matter how I framed it, I was part of the destruction.

No matter how I justified it, I knew in my gut I was contributing to someone else's suffering.

But that's the world we live in now.

A world where *nothing is really wrong anymore*.

Everything has an excuse.

Everything has a loophole.

Everything is just another personal choice, another way to "live your truth."

We tell ourselves that if no one gets caught, if we don't feel too guilty, it's fine.

Cheating. Porn. Casual sex. Drinking. Distractions.

None of it feels like a big deal.

None of it seems "evil."

But we've stopped asking the question that really matters:

Is it good for me?

> **"No man is free who cannot control himself."**
> —Pythagoras

NUMB IS THE NEW NORMAL

Somewhere along the way, we lost the ability to say no to ourselves.

We started confusing freedom with indulgence.

We started calling avoidance "self-care."

We started mistaking numbing for living.

It's easier to say yes.

Yes to the scroll.

Yes to the drink.

Yes to the momentary hit of pleasure that doesn't cost much… until it does.

And the culture rewards it.

Discipline is mocked. Pleasure is king.

If it feels good, it must *be* good.

If it's normalized, it must be *fine*.

But is it?

If it were, why are so many men walking around empty?

Why are addiction, depression, and anxiety climbing?

Why do we feel like something is missing, no matter how much we consume?

WHEN CONVENIENCE BECOMES A CAGE

Here's what I believe:

None of these things is inherently evil.

A drink now and then. A night of fun. A moment of indulgence.

They won't break you.

But the problem isn't the thing, it's the pattern.

The *autopilot*.

The unwillingness to ask: *Is this making me stronger?*

Porn is easy.

It offers the illusion of intimacy without effort.

No risk. No connection. No vulnerability. Just instant gratification.

And over time, it numbs you. It rewires you. It makes real connections feel harder than they should.

Casual sex is easy.

It gives you the rush, the ego boost, the illusion of connection.

But it doesn't build trust. It doesn't anchor love. It just fills the moment and leaves it emptier.

Drinking is easy.

Weed is easy.

Video games. Social media. Scrolling. All easy.

And that's the trap.

The world makes it easy to be passive.

To be entertained.

To be numb.

Because when you're distracted, you don't question.

When you're pacified, you don't lead.

When you're chasing cheap dopamine highs, you never stop to ask: *What am I really here for?*

And that's how they keep you stuck.

A numb man is easy to sell to.

A distracted man is easy to control.

A man who seeks only comfort will never challenge the system.

> **"I can resist everything except temptation."**
> —Oscar Wilde

REAL FREEDOM ISN'T WHAT YOU THINK

They won't tell you to stop.

They won't challenge your impulses.

They want you to stay on the loop.

Because real freedom? That's dangerous.

Real freedom is the ability to *choose*.

To say no to what doesn't serve you.

To break the cycle.

To walk away when every part of you wants to lean in.

Real freedom is not doing whatever you want.

It's being strong enough to do what you *need* to do, even when it's hard.

It's not the man who follows his every impulse who's free.

It's the man who knows how to master them.

I wish I could go back to that night at the bar.

Back to the moment my friend shrugged and said, "She'll never know."

Because I would have told him, "*You will.*"

And that's the only thing that really matters.

DAY 9 TASK: AUDIT YOUR PATTERNS

Take a hard, honest look at your daily life.

Ask yourself:

- What do I reach for when I'm bored, anxious, lonely, or disconnected?
- Which of my habits are easy, but weakening me?
- Which ones feel good in the moment but leave me emptier?

Write down one thing you know isn't serving you.

Then finish this sentence in your journal:

"If I were truly free, I would…"

Today, say no to that one thing.

Just for today.

Prove to yourself that *you* are the one in control.

THE BATTLE YOU DIDN'T KNOW YOU WERE FIGHTING

The moment you begin to teach, you become the example. And once you become the example, the war within shifts. Now you're no longer just fighting for yourself, you're fighting for every man watching.

Most people wake up every day and think they're just going through the motions: grabbing their coffee, heading to work, handling responsibilities.

They think they're just living life.

But they're wrong.

They're fighting a battle.

And most don't even realize they're losing.

Because this war isn't fought with bullets or swords.

It's fought with *choices*.

Every day, every moment, you are choosing what side you're on.

You are either building yourself into something stronger, sharper, more resilient,

or you are dulling yourself, weakening, letting the darkness creep in one small compromise at a time.

The problem is, most people have been armed with the wrong weapons.

The enemy doesn't come at you in some obvious way.

No one says, "*Hey, trade your discipline for distraction. Your focus for dopamine. Your health for convenience. I'll make sure you never reach your full potential.*"

No.

It's subtle.

It's a slow poison.

- The drink at the end of a long day that turns into three.
- The "just one more episode" that leaves you exhausted and behind.
- The scroll that numbs you out just enough to stop caring.
- The food that fills your stomach but fogs your mind.
- The fear that says, *Play it safe. Don't risk. Don't try.*

And the worst part?

It all feels normal.

Society tells you these things are fine.

Everyone does them. It's just part of life.

Relax, enjoy yourself. Don't take things so seriously.

But what they don't tell you is this:

Every one of those "normal" behaviors is a weapon.

Used *against* you.

Tools of weakness, disguised as freedom.

Chains, disguised as comfort.

And every time you pick them up, you have given away your power.

> **"It is no measure of health to be well adjusted to a profoundly sick society."**
> —Jiddu Krishnamurti

THE WEAPONS OF DARKNESS

The Devil doesn't show up in a red cape with a pitchfork.

He shows up in the small choices you don't question.

The ones that seem harmless, until they're not.

Alcohol and drugs are sold as "taking the edge off." But what are they really blunting?

Your clarity. Your fire. Your truth.

They keep you from facing the thing that needs to be faced- *you.*

Porn and cheap pleasure sell the illusion of connection but deliver only depletion.

No risk. No intimacy. No depth.

Just validation without value, and a growing inability to feel real connection.

Social media and endless scrolling pretend to entertain you, but they train your brain to need novelty, not meaning.

They keep you reactive rather than creative. Consuming instead of creating.

Fear-based thinking doesn't scream, it whispers:

You're not ready. You're not enough. You're too late.

It shrinks you from the inside out.

Weak food fuels a weak body.

A weak body builds a weak mind.

Garbage in, garbage out.

This is how the battle is lost; not in a single blow, but in a thousand quiet surrenders.

But there's another path.

And you can take it.

THE WEAPONS OF LIGHT

A warrior doesn't fight with broken weapons.

If what you've been using is making you weaker, it's time to change your arsenal.

Meditation and breathwork sharpen the mind.

You control your breath, you control your state.

You control your state, you control your choices.

Simple. Effective. Powerful.

Martial arts and physical training forge discipline.

Not just muscle. Mental armor.

When your body is strong, your mind learns how to carry weight.

You learn how to push through. How to finish. How to endure.

Books and deep thinking are weapons most men overlook.

If you don't feed your mind something strong, it will default to weakness.

A hungry mind will eat anything, and most of what's out there is poison.

Purpose and discipline are the core.

Without them, everything falls apart.

With them? You become dangerous in the best way possible.

THE PATH AHEAD

Up until now, you may not have realized you were in a war.

But now, you know.

And knowledge is power, but only if you use it.

In the next section, we're going to go deeper.

We'll break down the tools of darkness: **lust, greed, ego, fear, distraction**, and show you how they operate.

Then we'll walk through the weapons of light; the tools that will forge you into something stronger than you've ever been.

This isn't just about understanding.

It's about reclaiming your power.

Building your arsenal.

Choosing who you're going to become.

The battle is real.

The enemy is subtle.

But you?

You're no longer asleep.

Now it's time to fight for something more.

FINAL THOUGHT: CHOOSE YOUR ARSENAL

You don't rise by chance.

You rise by choice.

And the weapons you choose…

They'll either sharpen you or destroy you.

Pick them wisely.

DAY 10 TASK: INVENTORY YOUR ARSENAL

Tonight, take a quiet moment alone.

Write down two lists:

List 1: My Weapons of Weakness

Be brutally honest. What are you using to numb, avoid, escape, or self-sabotage?

List 2: My Weapons of Strength

What tools, habits, people, or practices make you stronger, clearer, more disciplined?

Then answer this:

> **Which list am I living from more often? And what needs to change-today?**

This isn't about shame.

It's about clarity.

And clarity is the first weapon of the warrior.

CHAPTER 11

THE DEVIL WITHIN

THE BATTLE WE ALL FIGHT

In Chapter 10, we opened our eyes to the war being waged in plain sight. But the truth is, the greatest enemy you'll face won't come from the outside. He lives inside you.

There's a voice inside us all. Some call it the Devil. Some call it the ego. Some say it's just human nature.

Whatever name we give it, we all know what it feels like.

It's the whisper that tells you to take more than you need, to put yourself above others, to chase validation at the cost of your soul.

It's the force that turns fear into paralysis, love into possession, hunger into greed.

And the most dangerous part?

It doesn't announce itself as evil.

It convinces you it's *necessary*.

It tells you that judgment is wisdom.

That greed is ambition.

That lust is freedom.

That ego is confidence.

That fear is protection.

And before you know it, you're serving something you don't even realize has taken control.

I've danced with all these demons in one way or another. We all have.

And every time I thought I had one beaten, another would step in to take its place.

This chapter isn't about condemning those forces.

It's about recognizing them, calling them out, and choosing something better.

Because the Devil within us isn't some outside enemy, it's the part of us that refuses to evolve.

JUDGMENT: THE ILLUSION OF SEPARATION

Judgment is the Devil's favorite trick because it feels so dang good.

It makes us feel superior.

It makes us feel safe in our own choices.

It makes us believe we're above the people we condemn.

I used to think I had people figured out.

I thought I knew what made someone weak, lazy, and undisciplined.

But life has a way of humbling you.

I've been knocked down.

I've lost things I thought I'd always have.

I've questioned everything I once believed.

And I started to see that the people I judged weren't so different from me.

Maybe they *were* me.

Maybe they *will be*.

What if the universe makes us live as those we judge, so we can finally learn empathy?

Judgment separates us.

It feeds the illusion that we're on different sides, when in truth, we're all in the same fight.

> **"Until you make the unconscious conscious, it will direct your life, and you will call it fate."**
> —Carl Jung

GREED: THE BOTTOMLESS PIT

Greed isn't just about money.

It's about **not enough**.

Not enough success.

Not enough admiration.

Not enough power.

And here's the tricky part:

Greed doesn't look evil from the inside. It looks like ambition. It looks like drive.

But it's a hole you can never fill.

Because greed isn't about what you have. It's about what you *think you lack*.

I've made money. I've lost money. And I've learned that **nothing external can make you whole if you're broken on the inside**.

Greed thrives when we believe something out there will finally make us feel like enough.

But nothing out there can.

LUST: THE ILLUSION OF FREEDOM

Lust tells you that giving in to every desire is liberation.

But there's a difference between owning your desire and being owned by it.

Lust is more than sex. It's the *search for something outside yourself* to avoid facing what's inside.

I've seen good men destroy themselves chasing the next high, the next conquest, the next hit of validation.

And like greed, it never satisfies.

You always come back to yourself.

And if you don't like who you are when you're alone, all the pleasure in the world won't change that.

EGO: THE NEED TO BE MORE

Ego is the Devil in disguise.

It wears the costume of success.

It whispers:

Be the best.

Prove them wrong.

Don't let anyone see you sweat.

I lived in that mindset for years, especially as a fighter.

Win. Dominate. Be the alpha.

But the ego's version of strength is just fear in a better outfit.

True power?

That's quiet.

It doesn't need applause.

It doesn't need to win.

It just *is*.

FEAR: THE SILENT KILLER

Fear is the foundation of them all.

Greed is the fear of lack.

Lust is the fear of emptiness.

The ego is the fear of insignificance.

Judgment is the fear of facing yourself in someone else.

I was raised to fear hell.

To fear failure.

To fear stepping outside the lines.

And for a long time, fear kept me small.

But what if *that's* the real hell?

Not fire and brimstone, but a life unlived.

A soul never tested.

A heart kept locked behind comfort and control.

THE ILLUSION OF COMPETITION

Since childhood, we're told that life is a race.

Be the best.

Outperform.

Outshine.

But most men are running a race they don't even want to win.

Real strength isn't about beating the guy next to you.

It's about beating who you were yesterday.

Because the reality is, **you are not in competition with anyone else.**

THE CHOICE WE FACE

Every day, we stand at a crossroads.

One path leads to destruction, judgment, greed, lust, ego, and fear.

The other leads to freedom.

But the Devil doesn't show up in an obvious way.

He shows up in your desires.

In your need to be liked.

In your moments of weakness disguised as strength.

The moment you see the game, you start to win it.

FINAL THOUGHT: THE BATTLE WE MUST FIGHT

This isn't about blaming something outside of you for what's gone wrong.

It's about owning what lives inside of you.

The part that chooses fear or courage. Ego or truth. Lust or love.

We are all God.

We are all the Devil.

And every single day, we decide who we serve.

DAY 11 TASK: NAME THE DEVIL

Today, take a moment to sit in silence and write down:

- Which of these forces, judgment, greed, lust, ego, or fear, shows up most in your life?
- What does it cost you?
- Who could you become if you stopped feeding it?

Then finish this sentence in your journal:

"Today, I choose to stop serving ___, and start becoming ___."

Read it out loud.

Own it.

That's how you reclaim your power.

CHAPTER 12

THE WAR INSIDE

In the last chapter, we named the Devil. Not as some creature in the shadows, but as the voice inside us, the one that feeds on fear, ego, lust, and self-doubt. Now it's time to go to war with it.

People spend their whole lives fearing the Devil.

They picture a shadowy figure lurking in the dark, waiting to drag them down.

But what if the Devil isn't *out there*?

What if he's already *inside*?

What if he's the voice that whispers:

- *You're not good enough.*
- *You'll never measure up.*
- *This is just who you are. Give up.*

And what if God isn't some distant being in the clouds, but the quiet voice that rises *within* you?

The one that says:

- *Stand up.*
- *Fight.*
- *Be better.*

The war isn't happening in some distant realm.

It's happening right now, inside you.

In every choice you make.

THE CHOICES THAT SHAPE YOU

Some choices feel small.

Do you hit snooze or get up and train?

Do you eat clean or cave to comfort?

Do you numb yourself with distraction or face your pain head-on?

But some choices define your life.

I faced one of those moments at just 23 years old.

My son Trent's mother was killed in a car accident.

He was only eight months old.

Suddenly, I wasn't just a father, I was *his only parent.*

And I was terrified.

I was young. I had no idea what I was doing.

Worse, I wasn't married to his mother. Her parents wanted custody.

Then came the offer:

"If you sign over your parental rights, you won't have to pay child support."

I could have walked away.

No courtroom battles. No financial burden. No responsibility.

And for a second, I thought about it.

Wouldn't this be easier?

You're too young. You're not ready.

Just move on. Start over.

That was the Devil's voice.

The voice that offers *comfort in exchange for your soul.*

But then came another voice.

Quieter. Steadier. Stronger.

There is no choice. This is your son. You show up.

And I did.

Even though I didn't get full custody, I drove two and a half hours each way, every other weekend, just to be with him.

I built that relationship brick by brick, through every obstacle, every mile, every hard decision.

That battle wasn't fought in a courtroom.

It was fought in my mind.

And that's how the war works.

The Devil offers comfort.

God offers responsibility.

One weakens you.

The other *builds you into who you're meant to be.*

> **"The line separating good and evil passes not through states, nor between classes, nor between political parties either—but right through every human heart."**
> —Aleksandr Solzhenitsyn

THE MIND IS THE TRUE BATTLEFIELD

Most people think the battle only shows up in big moments.

But it's happening *every day* in the smallest decisions.

- When you wake up feeling unmotivated, what voice are you listening to?
- Who is whispering back when you say, '*I'll start tomorrow*'?
- When fear shows up and tells you to back down, whose game are you playing?

The voice of God pushes you forward:

- *Go.*
- *Grow.*
- *Lead.*
- *Create.*

The voice of the Devil pulls you backward:

- *You're not ready.*
- *Stay safe.*
- *What if you fail?*
- *Just one more excuse.*

And the worst part?

Most people think the Devil's voice is *their own.*

THE GREATEST TRICK THE DEVIL EVER PULLED

You've heard it said:

The greatest trick the Devil ever pulled was convincing the world he didn't exist.

But I'll go one step further:

The greatest trick the Devil ever pulled was convincing you that his voice was your own.

That's how he wins.

He doesn't need to destroy you.

He just needs you to doubt yourself.

To question your power.

To believe that weakness, fear, and self-sabotage are your truth.

But the moment you realize that voice isn't *you*, you take your power back.

The war inside you? It's real.

But so is the victory.

FINAL THOUGHT: VICTORY IS A DAILY CHOICE

This isn't about waiting for some holy moment where you're suddenly fearless and perfect.

It's about choosing today, right now, to stop believing the voice that keeps you stuck and small.

You know the truth.

You've heard the other voice, the one that calls you higher.

Now it's time to answer it.

DAY 12 TASK: IDENTIFY THE VOICE

Today, pay attention to your thoughts.

When resistance shows up, when fear or self-doubt creeps in, pause and ask:

- Is this voice pulling me forward or holding me back?
- Is it truth or fear?
- Is this the voice of God or the voice of the Devil?

Then write this in your journal and finish it:

> **"The Devil's voice in my life often sounds like ___. I choose instead to listen to ___."**

This is the war.

Win it one decision at a time.

CHAPTER 13

THE PRISON OF THE MIND

You've seen the Devil's disguise. You've heard the voice inside that keeps you trapped. Now it's time to confront the cage he's built around you and realize the key has been in your hand all along.

Most people think of prison as a physical place: steel bars, locked doors, and concrete walls that keep a man from his freedom. But the most powerful prisons aren't built from brick and mortar. They don't need guards or fences. They live in the mind, invisible and unbreakable to those who don't even realize they're trapped.

And that's the crazy part. Most people don't know they're locked inside.

The walls of this prison aren't made of concrete. They're built from doubt, fear, and hesitation. A man might look free; he has a good job, a strong body, a loving partner, but inside, he's chained to thoughts that keep him from stepping fully into his life.

What if I fail?

What will people think?

What if I'm not good enough?

These aren't just passing thoughts. They're bars, each one forged by years of conditioning, old wounds, past failures. And like any prison, the longer you stay inside, the more it starts to feel like home.

> **"Man is not worried by real problems so much as by his imagined anxieties about real problems."**
> —Epictetus

THE PRISON WITH OPEN DOORS

At my retreats, I've met men who, on the surface, have everything. They're successful, disciplined, and in great shape. They have money in the bank, a beautiful home, maybe even a family they love. From the outside, they look like the kind of men others envy.

And yet, time and time again, they tell me the same thing.

"I feel stuck."

It doesn't make sense at first. How can a man with so many options, so much potential, feel trapped? But then it clicks. They have too many options. And instead of taking action, they freeze.

They could do anything. So instead, they do nothing.

It's like they're standing in a wide-open prison cell, the door unlocked, the path to freedom right in front of them. But they won't step through. Not because they can't, but because they're afraid of what's on the other side.

THE THIRD RESPONSE: FIGHT, FLIGHT... OR FREEZE

Most people know about the fight-or-flight response, the body's response to danger. When faced with a threat, you either stand your ground and fight or you run. But there's a third response most people don't talk about: freeze.

A deer in the headlights. A fighter who hesitates for just a second too long and gets knocked out. A man who spends his days overthinking instead of acting.

He's afraid of choosing the wrong thing, so he chooses nothing.

What if I pick the wrong path?

What if I fail and can't recover?

What if I was meant to do something else?

The thoughts loop in his mind, over and over, keeping him stuck. And he doesn't even realize that standing still is its own kind of failure.

Another thing I often say in my self-defense classes during our stress drills is, "Anticipation, without confirmation, leads to hesitation." We think something is going to happen, i.e., an attack, when our eyes are closed, and we brace for it, but it hasn't happened yet, and then we hesitate. Or, maybe it's a promotion, a new relationship, or something bad even, and we become trapped in the moment, waiting.

THE FEAR OF CHOOSING WRONG

The real prison isn't a lack of opportunity. It's the fear of making the wrong choice.

A man without options feels trapped. But a man with too many options often becomes just as stuck.

The fear of picking a business idea and watching it crash.

The fear of committing to a path and realizing too late that it wasn't the right one.

The fear of walking away from a comfortable but unfulfilling life and having no safety net.

So instead of choosing something, he chooses nothing. Paralysis by analysis. Some men spend their whole lives trapped here. And life, unlike a patient teacher, doesn't wait. It moves forward whether you do or not.

HOW TO BREAK OUT: THE POWER OF CHOOSING SOMETHING

The fastest way out of this kind of prison? Pick a path and commit.

Even if it's not the perfect choice, momentum creates clarity. A man doesn't think his way into purpose; he acts his way into it.

I've seen this play out in fighting time and time again. The guys who hesitate, who wait for the "perfect" opening, who overthink every movement, they get knocked out. You can't calculate your way to victory. At some point, you must throw the first punch.

Life works the same way.

You don't sit in a room and think your way to clarity. You step forward, you take action, and through the experience of doing, you figure out if you're on the right path. And if you're not? You adjust. But at least you're moving.

NO MORE FREEZING

If you feel stuck, ask yourself:

If I had to make a move today, what would I do?

If I knew I couldn't fail, what choice would I make?

The door is open. The only thing keeping you inside is you.

Because the worst decision isn't choosing wrong.

It's choosing nothing at all.

The mind might build the prison, but courage is always the key. And as we begin dismantling the forces that built these walls, you'll see how each one has been keeping you from the man you're meant to be.

DAY 13 TASK: BREAK THE LOOP

Today, name the prison.

Ask yourself:

- Where in my life do I feel stuck?
- What decision am I avoiding because I'm afraid of getting it wrong?

Write this in your journal:

"If I weren't afraid of failing, I would…"

Then take one small step toward that thing today.

Don't overthink it. Don't wait for permission.

Throw the first punch.

Momentum is your jailbreak.

CHAPTER 14

PERCEPTION IS REALITY

THE KISMET STORY

When you finally throw the first punch and take a step out of the mental prison, something surprising happens: the world doesn't instantly reward you. Sometimes, it throws you another test. A closed door. A curveball. A reminder that just because you moved doesn't mean the path will be smooth. That's the real test of freedom: how you respond when things don't go your way.

It's funny how life unfolds.

Sometimes you think you know exactly where you're going, only to find yourself somewhere completely different. And when that happens, you're left with a choice: do you see it as failure or redirection? A loss or a hidden gift?

When I bought Casas Kismet, I believed I was also securing the adjoining property. The deal seemed solid, the vision was clear, and in my mind, it was already mine. But when the sale fell through, everything changed.

For a moment, frustration took over.

Had I miscalculated? Had I lost an opportunity that was meant to be mine? I had already seen the expansion, imagined the potential, felt the certainty of it. And yet, the door had closed before I could step through.

That's when the real question surfaced.

Was I being protected from something I couldn't yet see? Was this a moment of divine intervention, keeping me from taking on too much?

Or was this a test? A challenge to see if I truly wanted it badly enough to fight harder?

> **"Be content with what you have; rejoice in the way things are. When you realize there is nothing lacking, the whole world belongs to you."**
> —Tao Te Ching

THE STRUGGLE: BE HAPPY WITH WHAT YOU HAVE, OR STRIVE FOR MORE?

This is the eternal battle, isn't it?

The fine line between contentment and ambition.

Some people never stop chasing, convinced that happiness exists just beyond the next achievement. Others convince themselves that wanting more is dangerous, so they settle, telling themselves at peace, when their soul knows they're just playing small.

Which one was I supposed to be?

If I accepted that the deal fell through for a reason, did that mean I should surrender and trust that this was all I was meant to have?

Or was I supposed to push harder, refuse to accept "no," and fight until I got what I wanted?

This wasn't just about land.

This was about everything.

How do you know when to surrender?

And how do you know when to push forward?

TRUE ABUNDANCE—WANTING MORE VS. NEEDING LESS

We've been conditioned to believe that abundance means *more.*

More money. More possessions. More power. More everything.

It's the lie that keeps men sprinting toward a finish line that keeps moving. They think if they could just add one more thing, another zero in the bank, another deal, another body in bed, *then* they'd finally feel like enough.

But you've seen it. So have I.

Men with everything who feel like they have nothing.

Men with nothing who radiate peace.

That's because real abundance doesn't come from stacking things.

It comes from shedding what you don't need.

> **"He is richest who is content with the least, for content is the wealth of nature."**
> —Socrates

THE POWER OF WANTING NOTHING

Think about it.

If you need nothing, what can be taken from you?

If you desire nothing outside of yourself, what can control you?

Most men don't want abundance. They want relief.

They want peace.

They want to feel like they're enough.

But instead of looking inward, they chase outward. They hope the next purchase, the next promotion, the next victory will silence the nagging voice inside.

It never does.

Because the voice doesn't want you to win more.

It wants you to *listen more.*

And the men who walk into a room with real presence, the ones who don't need to prove anything? They're not empty.

They're *full.*

ABUNDANCE VS. SCARCITY—
THE REAL CHOICE

This isn't about rejecting wealth or success.

It's about breaking your attachment to them.

A weak man lives in fear of losing what he has.

A strong man knows he's the source of everything he builds.

A weak man clings.

A strong man lets go.

That's the real power.

Not in how much you hold, but how much you can release.

THE UNSTOPPABLE MAN

A man who can manifest anything is dangerous.

But a man who *needs* nothing?

He is untouchable.

Because you can't buy him.

You can't manipulate him.

You can't own him.

And that's the kind of man the world can't break.

> **"When you realize there is nothing lacking,
> the whole world belongs to you."**
> —Lao Tzu

THE LESSON: PERCEPTION
SHAPES EVERYTHING

Sometimes you don't get what you want.

Sometimes you don't get what you think you need.

And sometimes, that's the blessing.

Other times, you must fight like hell to claim it.

Mastery isn't about always surrendering. It's not about always chasing either.

It's about knowing when to rest and when to rise.

When to flow and when to fight.

And how do you know which is which?

Trust.

Trust the timing.

Trust the process.

Trust yourself.

Because abundance doesn't come from what you collect.

It comes from what you believe you already are.

DAY 14 TASK: RECLAIM ABUNDANCE

Today, take 15 minutes to reflect on where in your life you're operating from a place of *scarcity.*

Ask yourself:

- Where am I afraid of losing something?
- Where am I chasing validation, success, or comfort instead of trusting what I already have?
- What would it look like to let go of that fear today?

Now write this sentence and finish it:

> **"If I truly believed I already have enough, I would stop chasing ___ and start creating ___."**

Say it out loud.

Say it like it's already true.

That's how abundance begins.

Join Us at Casas Kismet

CHAPTER 15

CHOOSE CREATION OVER CONSUMPTION

You can either build your own world or be distracted by someone else's.

The modern world isn't designed to make you strong. It's designed to keep you consume: scrolling through social media, watching endless shows, eating food with no nutrition, and absorbing news designed to make you anxious. Everywhere you turn, someone is trying to sell you something.

And here's what I believe to be true: the more you consume, the weaker you become. The more you create, the stronger you become.

That's the difference between men who lead and men who stay stuck.

Ask yourself one simple question: are you creating more than you consume?

> **"To live is the rarest thing in the world.**
> **Most people exist, that is all."**
> —Oscar Wilde

CONSUMPTION KEEPS YOU WEAK

It happens so easily, you don't even notice. You think you're unwinding, killing time, staying "informed." But in reality, you're just being fed distractions.

The more you consume, the more reactive you become. Instead of creating your own path, you're just responding to whatever the world throws at you. You stay addicted to instant gratification, getting little dopamine hits from scrolling, eating, or watching, but nothing that moves you forward.

Worst of all, you lose time. Hours disappear in front of screens, and you wonder why you never seem to have enough time to build the life you want.

And that's the trap. Most men don't even realize it's happening. They think they're making progress, but they're just watching other people live their lives.

If you're always consuming, you're never creating. And if you're never creating, you're never in control.

CREATION MAKES YOU POWERFUL

The moment you shift from consumer to creator, everything changes.

You build momentum, small creations add up, whether it's a business, a skill, or your body. You take control of your time, shaping the world instead of reacting to it. And most importantly, you generate real fulfillment. Watching someone else's success feels empty. Building your own gives you purpose.

Creation is where power is built.

And it doesn't matter what you create.

You can build a stronger body, write, journal, create content, start a business, learn an instrument, or teach and inspire others. The act of creation itself is what sets you apart. The moment you start creating, you start leading.

Every minute spent creating makes you stronger. Every minute spent consuming makes you weaker. Choose wisely.

HOW I GOT STUCK IN CONSUMPTION

I know how easy it is to fall into this trap.

There was a time when I let consumption take control of me.

It started as something innocent, playing video games with my sons, Trent and Jdub. At first, it was great. Even when they weren't with me, we could still talk, laugh, and bond over the game. It felt like time well spent.

But over time, something shifted.

Even when I wasn't playing with them, I kept playing.

I'd tell myself, "Just one more round," but that round would turn into an hour. Then two. I'd catch myself staying up late, playing alone, wasting hours that could have been spent building something real.

And that's when it hit me.

I wasn't just playing to connect with my kids anymore. I was playing because it was an easy escape.

The moment I realized that, I made a hard rule.

I deleted the games from my phone. I removed the temptation completely.

Not because video games are evil. But because I knew myself. I knew that if they were accessible, I'd keep getting sucked back in. And the only way to reclaim my time was to make creation easier than consumption.

THE SHIFT—MOVING FROM CONSUMER TO CREATOR

Breaking free isn't about eliminating all consumption. It's about making sure creation always comes first.

If you watch, read, or listen to something, use it as fuel to build something of your own. If you spend time on social media, create more than you consume. If you play video games or watch TV, set strict limits so it doesn't control you.

At the end of the day, ask yourself one question:

Did I create more than I consumed today?

If the answer is no, adjust.

The world doesn't need more consumers. It needs more creators. The choice is yours.

The man who chooses perception over panic, who sees meaning in redirection instead of failure, is the same man who eventually realizes he was never meant to just absorb life. He was meant to shape it. And the moment you accept that, you stop watching and start building.

DAY 15 TASK: BUILD SOMETHING TODAY

Pick one thing to create today. It doesn't have to be big.

Write a page. Record a video. Cook a meal. Start a workout plan. Have a meaningful conversation.

Whatever it is, make it yours.

Then journal this:

> **"Today I chose to create instead of consuming.
> I built _______. And it made me feel _______."**

Tomorrow, build again. Even just one brick.

Creators build kingdoms. Consumers just rent space in someone else's.

CHAPTER 16

FACE DISCOMFORT HEAD-ON

If you run from discomfort, you run from growth.

Most men avoid discomfort. They stay where it's safe, where it's easy, where they won't be challenged. They convince themselves that staying comfortable is the smart thing to do, the logical choice. But deep down, they know the truth.

Growth and comfort cannot exist in the same space.

Everything you want is on the other side of something hard.

Pain isn't the enemy. It's the path.

If you never put yourself in uncomfortable situations, you never evolve.

A man who avoids struggle also avoids strength.

WHY WE AVOID DISCOMFORT

Most men aren't weak.

They're just untested.

The modern world makes it too easy to stay soft.

Food is always available, so you never have to go hungry.

Entertainment is instant, so you never have to sit with boredom.

Comfort is everywhere, so you never have to struggle for survival.

And because of that, so many men feel lost.

They were built to fight, to endure, to overcome.

But they live in a world where they never have to.

So they stay safe. They avoid pain. They get stuck.

The world has made life easy.

But an easy life makes weak men.

> **"The obstacle is the way."**
> —Marcus Aurelius

THE TRUTH ABOUT PAIN & STRUGGLE

Pain isn't something to avoid. It's something to lean into.

When your body is in pain from training, it's growing stronger.

When your mind is in pain from pushing your limits, it's becoming sharper.

When your heart is in pain from failure, it's learning resilience.

Pain is the price of progress.

Struggle isn't a punishment. It's a gift.

Because the man who struggles is the man who rises.

THE UMBRELLA THAT TAUGHT ME A LESSON

Not all pain is about physical struggle.

Some of it is about emotional control.

Last year, I was in a rush to get my retreat guests to dinner. The wind was picking up, and I was trying to bring the cushions inside before the rain hit. That's when the umbrella folded inside out.

I was frustrated. In a hurry. Irritated.

Without thinking, I grabbed it and snapped it in half.

The second I did, I knew I had messed up.

The broken edge sliced my middle finger wide open.

Fourteen stitches later, I still don't have feeling in that finger.

Now, every time I look at it, I'm reminded of one thing:

A moment of lost control can leave a permanent mark.

And honestly, I feel blessed that a numb finger and a scar are all that happened!

Pain is a teacher, but you don't always get to choose the lesson.

You can either learn through discipline or through destruction.

The man who builds begins by creating. The man who endures begins by choosing pain on purpose. Chapter 15 taught us to step away from consumption and into creation. But real creation? It demands discomfort. It demands struggle. And when you stop fearing pain and start respecting it, you become unstoppable.

DAY 16 TASK: SEEK DISCOMFORT ON PURPOSE

Today, do one thing that challenges you physically, emotionally, or mentally.

- Train until it burns.
- Start the hard conversation.
- Sit in silence with your discomfort.

Then write in your journal:

> **"The discomfort I faced today was _______.**
> **Here's what it taught me: _______."**

Pain isn't punishment.

It's proof you're getting stronger.

Let it sharpen you, not break you.

CHAPTER 17

RESPONDING TO TRAGEDY

FINDING PURPOSE IN PAIN

You can learn from discomfort. But what happens when pain doesn't make sense? When it blindsides you, not as a challenge, but as devastation? In Chapter 16, we leaned into the pain we chose. Now we face the pain we never asked for. This is where strength is forged on a soul-deep level, not in the gym, but in the wreckage of life.

Some pain makes sense.

You train hard, you wake up sore.

You push yourself. You feel discomfort.

That kind of pain is easy to understand. It has a clear cause and a clear result.

But then there's the other kind.

The kind of pain that blindsides you.

That doesn't make sense.

That rips through your life like a wrecking ball, leaving nothing but destruction in its path.

And that kind of pain forces you to make a choice.

You can let it break you.

Or you can let it build you.

Most people don't realize they have that choice.

They think pain is just something that happens to them. A curse. A punishment. A cruel joke from the universe.

But the truth is, **suffering is a tool**.

The Devil uses it to break men.

God uses it to build them.

The question is, **who will you let shape you?**

MARCUS'S LOSS AND MY OWN EXPERIENCE WITH DRUNK DRIVING TRAGEDY

I've seen firsthand how tragedy can either destroy a man or turn him into something stronger. My longtime friend and business partner Marcus knows this truth better than most.

Marcus was a fighter, just like me. He knew what it meant to push through pain, to endure, to keep moving forward. But nothing could have prepared him for the day his 15-month-old son, Liam, was killed by a drunk driver.

A parent's worst nightmare.

The kind of pain no one can ever be ready for.

Most men would never recover from something like that. Most would shut down, disappear, or drown themselves in rage, alcohol, or anything else that could numb the weight of that loss.

But Marcus didn't.

He turned his pain into a mission. He created Liam's Life Foundation, dedicated to fighting drunk driving and making sure no other parent has to experience what he did.

He turned his suffering into service.

And in that, he found purpose.

I've felt that kind of pain too.

I've stood in the aftermath of a drunk driving tragedy.

I've looked at the wreckage, felt the anger, the confusion, the helplessness.

And I know the truth, when life hits you that hard, it changes you.

The only question is:

Will you let it destroy you, or will you use it?

DO BAD THINGS HAPPEN RANDOMLY, OR DO THEY SERVE A HIGHER PURPOSE?

This is the question that keeps men up at night.

When the unthinkable happens…

When life delivers suffering that seems meaningless…

Most people spiral.

They ask, *why me?*

They look for someone to blame.

They let their pain fester into anger, bitterness, and despair.

But what if pain isn't meaningless?

What if every tragedy carries within it the seed of transformation?

What if the worst thing that ever happened to you is also the thing that could push you to become the man you were meant to be?

I'm not saying the pain is justified.

I'm not saying it's fair.

I'm saying it's fuel.

And the only difference between the men who rise and the men who fall **is whether they choose to use it.**

> **"He who has a why to live can bear almost any how."**
> —Friedrich Nietzsche

THE CHOICE: LET SUFFERING BREAK YOU, OR LET IT BUILD YOU

Pain is inevitable.

Suffering is universal.

There is no man alive who will not, at some point, be brought to his knees by life.

But the outcome?

That's up to you.

You can let the pain make you bitter,

Or you can let it make you better.

You can let it turn you into a victim,

Or you can let it turn you into a warrior.

You can let it shut you down,

Or you can let it set you on fire.

The greatest men in history were not the ones who lived easy lives.

They were the ones who suffered, and instead of crumbling, they turned their suffering into something greater.

Marcus didn't choose what happened to him.

But he chose what he did with it.

You won't always have control over the pain life throws your way.

But you will always have control over your response.

Let it break you,

Or let it build you.

The choice is yours.

When pain knocks the wind out of you, you don't need to have the answers right away. But you *do* need to respond. Chapter 16 taught us that pain can sharpen you when you lean into it. But this kind of suffering? It calls you to something even greater: purpose. It's your move now.

DAY 17 TASK: TURN PAIN INTO PURPOSE

Reflect on the deepest pain or loss you've experienced.

Ask yourself:

- What strength did that moment call out of me?
- What did I learn that could serve someone else?

Now finish this sentence in your journal:

"Because of what I've been through, I can help others by…"

Your suffering wasn't random.

It's a weapon now, if you choose to wield it.

CHAPTER 18

STOP WAITING—THE TIME IS NOW

If Chapter 17 taught us anything, it's that life doesn't ask permission before it breaks you. Pain arrives without warning. Tragedy doesn't knock. So what are you waiting for? If you've felt the sting of loss, the ache of regret, the weight of wasted time, then you already know the truth. There is no later. There's only now.

Most men spend their lives waiting.

They wait for the right moment.

The perfect opportunity.

The stars to align.

They convince themselves that patience is a virtue, that timing is everything, that one day, when things settle down, when conditions improve, when the fear finally goes away, they'll take action.

But waiting is nothing more than slow-motion failure.

Every time you say, *"I'll start next week"* or *"I just need a little more time,"* you're lying to yourself.

You're not preparing.

You're stalling.

You're wasting time you will never get back.

Here's the brutal truth: **you're not promised tomorrow.**

Most men will die waiting for the "right time."

But the right time never comes.

THE LIE OF THE 'PERFECT TIME'

Society has sold you the fantasy of perfect timing.

You imagine a golden moment when everything clicks:

Your finances are stable.

Your energy is high.

Your confidence is unshakable.

But that moment?

It doesn't exist.

There is no perfect time.

There is no perfect plan.

There is no "ready."

If you don't take action today, you won't take action tomorrow.

If you don't start building now, you never will.

The life you want isn't coming to find you.

You have to go take it.

WHY I ALWAYS TAKE THE MEETING

One of the biggest lessons I've learned in life…

Always take the meeting.

I can't tell you how many opportunities came my way that I almost ignored.

It didn't seem like the right fit.

It wasn't what I was looking for.

It didn't feel like it was "meant for me."

But I took the meeting anyway.

And every time, something happened.

A door opened.

A connection was made.

A conversation sparked an idea that changed everything.

You never know who you'll meet.

You never know what path will be revealed.

You never know which small moment will be the one that shifts your entire future.

Most people settle for "good enough" too early in life.

They stay where it's safe, comfortable, familiar.

But I refused.

I started businesses before I was "ready."

I moved to Costa Rica when it didn't make sense on paper.

I created a retreat center I hadn't planned to own.

Every major move I made wasn't because I had it all figured out.

It was because I said yes to the moment.

Because I took the meeting.

> **"It is not that we have a short time to live,
> but that we waste a lot of it."**
> —Seneca

THE TRAP OF WAITING—FEAR IN DISGUISE

Most men don't wait because they're strategic.

They wait because they're scared.

Fear of failure: *What if I mess up?*

Fear of judgment: *What will people think?*

Fear of change: *What if it doesn't work out?*

And here's the thing, **fear doesn't shrink when you stall.**

It grows.

The more you hesitate, the louder it gets.

The longer you wait, the harder it gets to move.

You don't need more time.

You need more courage.

THE TIME IS NOW—TAKE THE SHOT

What's one thing you know you need to do, but you've been putting off?

- Starting the business?
- Having the hard conversation?
- Taking your health seriously?
- Leaving the comfort zone that's quietly killing you?

Stop waiting. Take the shot.

The world is full of men who waited too long.

Men who died with dreams still inside them.

Men who buried their potential under fear and excuses.

You are either stepping forward…

Or staying stuck.

There is no in-between.

The time is NOW.

You don't need a sign.

You don't need a roadmap.

You don't need someone's permission.

You need a decision.

Because in the next chapter, we're going to face the biggest lie of all: the illusion of time.

DAY 18 TASK: DO THE THING YOU'VE BEEN AVOIDING

Ask yourself:

- What is the ONE thing I know I need to do, but have been putting off?
- What am I waiting for that doesn't exist?

Now, do one bold thing today that moves you closer to it.

Call. Apply. Write. Launch. Start.

Doesn't matter how small, just move.

Then write this sentence in your journal:

"Today, I chose action over excuses. Today, I moved."

Say it out loud.

Because once you stop waiting, **your life begins.**

CHAPTER 19

CREATING YOUR REALITY

THE POWER YOU FORGOT YOU HAD

If Chapter 18 reminded you that waiting is the enemy, then this chapter is your reminder that creating is the answer. Once you stop stalling and start moving, the real shift begins you remember you've been the architect all along.

THE TURNING POINT—CHOOSING THE LIGHT

You've seen the weapons of darkness. You've felt them. Maybe they've even had a hold on you.

The distractions. The addictions. The fear. The lies that keep you weak, doubting yourself, waiting for someone else to change your life.

But now, you know better.

The Devil doesn't show up with horns. He shows up with comfort. Excuses. The easy way out.

And most men take it.

But not you.

If you're still here, it means you're ready. You're ready to become the kind of man who leads, not the one who waits.

Because the truth is simple:

A man ruled by darkness is controlled.

A man who walks in the light creates.

He builds. He leads. He takes responsibility.

And above all, **he remembers that he has the power.**

You will still battle the dark. That war never ends.

But now, we shift weapons.

Now, we begin to build.

Now we start creating a life so rooted in strength, discipline, clarity, and light that there's no shadow left to hide in.

YOUR LIFE ISN'T HAPPENING TO YOU—IT'S HAPPENING BECAUSE OF YOU

Most people drift through life thinking they're at the mercy of fate.

"That's just how life is."

"I'm unlucky."

"Nothing ever works out for me."

They speak these lies like gospel, like their lives were carved in stone.

But what if none of that is true?

What if your life is not *happening to you*, but *through you*?

What if everything around you, your money, your relationships, your habits, your mindset, is the result of what's happening inside your own mind?

Here's the truth:

> You're already creating your reality, whether you realize it or not.

The only question is, are you creating on purpose or by accident?

THE UNIVERSE IS MENTAL

Ancient traditions knew this long before science caught up:

> **"As a man thinketh in his heart, so is he."**
> —Proverbs 23:7
>
> **"If you have faith as small as a mustard seed...
> nothing will be impossible for you."**
> —Matthew 17:20
>
> **"The All is Mind."**
> —Hermetic Principle

Hinduism, Taoism, Buddhism, and Christianity all point to the same idea:

Your thoughts shape your world.

You don't just interpret reality.

You create it.

SCIENCE IS FINALLY CATCHING UP

Quantum physics has proven that particles behave differently when observed.

Your attention changes outcomes.

The placebo effect shows that belief alone can heal the body.

The mind rewires matter.

You are not a passive being.

You are not a product of your circumstances.

You are the creator.

HOW I MANIFESTED MY LIFE IN COSTA RICA

I was born in Weaverville, North Carolina. Small town. No passports. No grand plans.

My father never flew on a plane. My mom took her first flight here to see me last year at age 70.

The idea of living in Costa Rica, running a retreat center, building something that changes lives?

Unimaginable.

But I believed something different.

Even as a kid, I carried this unshakable belief:

"If I want it, I'll find a way."

I visualized the life I wanted before I ever had a clue how to make it happen.

And I didn't wait until it was logical. Even though I'm not really a surfer, or swimmer, I don't even get in the ocean that much, I always knew I wanted to live somewhere close to the beach. And then one day it happened…

I moved. I trusted. I created.

When I named the center **Casas Kismet**, it wasn't by accident.

Kismet means fate. Destiny.

And I believed, **every step led me here.**

Not luck. Not chance.

Creation.

THE POWER OF WORDS—SPEAK IT INTO EXISTENCE

Words aren't just sounds.

They're commands.

> **"Let there be light."**
> —Genesis 1:3
>
> **"Death and life are in the power of the tongue."**
> —Proverbs 18:21

Your language is either a weapon of creation or destruction.

Every time you say, "I'm not good enough," you reinforce that truth.

Every time you say, "I am powerful," your world begins to rise to meet it.

Speak what you want into existence.

Declare your life before it shows up.

MY MORNING MANTRA

For years, I spoke like most people, without intention.

Until I learned the truth.

Now, I start every single morning with this:

"My family and I are blessed and protected. We expand in love, abundance, success, and health every day, and we inspire others to do the same."

This isn't just a feel-good habit. It's a *command* to my subconscious.

It tells my mind what to build.

It overrides fear.

It calibrates my reality.

And it works.

> **"Man is not the creature of circumstances;**
> **circumstances are the creatures of men."**
> —Benjamin Disraeli

START CREATING; NOW

Here's how to begin:

1. Stop playing the victim.

No more "I can't."

No more "I'm stuck."

No more "This is just how life is."

2. Speak what you want.

Write it down. Speak it out loud.

Use the present tense. Say, "I am building a life I love."

Not "I hope someday…"

3. Take inspired action.

Creation demands movement.

Even one small step toward your vision ignites momentum.

THE TRUTH YOU MUST REMEMBER

You are not a slave to fate.

You are not powerless.

You are not broken.

You are a creator.

You are a builder.

You are a warrior of light.

Your thoughts, your words, and your actions, they shape your reality.

Every day, you choose.

Heaven or hell.

Destruction or creation.

Fear or power.

The choice has always been yours.

DAY 19 TASK: SPEAK IT AND STEP INTO IT

1. Write down a mantra that reflects the life you are creating. Example: *"I am grounded, powerful, disciplined, and I create a life of strength and peace."*
2. Say it out loud **three times** today: once in the morning, once midday, once before bed. Say it with conviction.
3. Take one small action that aligns with this new reality. Build. Move. Speak. Lead. Don't just write the words, **back them up.**

Then journal this sentence:

"Today, I created my reality on purpose."

Say it again tomorrow.

And the next day.

Until your reality matches your voice.

THE DISCIPLINE OF GRATITUDE

> **"Gratitude is not only the greatest of virtues,**
> **but the parent of all others."**
> —Cicero

Before I say anything else in the morning, before affirmations, before intentions, before planning the day, I start with gratitude.

Not because it sounds nice. Not because it's trendy. But because it immediately resets my perspective.

Before I ask God for anything, I acknowledge what's already been given.

Most people wake up and go straight into a state of lack. What needs to be done. What's wrong? What they didn't get yesterday. What they're worried about losing. That mindset hijacks the nervous system before your feet even hit the floor.

Gratitude does the opposite.

It grounds you in reality. Not imagined fears. Not future stress. Reality.

When I start naming what I'm grateful for, something interesting happens. I realize pretty quickly that I'm not short on blessings. I'm swimming in them.

Breath in my lungs. A body that still moves. A bed. A roof. Clean water. People who love me. Work that matters. The chance to wake up and try again.

That's not positive thinking. That's honesty.

Gratitude isn't pretending life is perfect. It's refusing to ignore what's already good.

And here's the part most people miss: gratitude is not passive. It's an active discipline. You have to choose it, especially on the hard days, especially when things feel uncertain, especially when your ego wants to complain.

When you name what you're grateful for out loud, you shift authority. You stop letting circumstances define your inner state. You take responsibility for where your attention goes.

I don't rush this practice. I don't mentally check boxes. I actually feel it. I let it land in my body. That's important. Gratitude that stays in your head doesn't change much. Gratitude that's felt rewires you.

Only after that do I move into affirmations.

Because affirmations without gratitude can turn into ego games. You're trying to build something on top of a shaky foundation. Gratitude reminds you that God has already been providing long before you started asking.

It humbles you. And humility is power.

When you genuinely recognize how much you've already been given, something else shifts. You stop approaching life as if it owes you something. You start approaching it like a steward. Like someone who's been trusted with a lot and wants to honor that trust.

That changes how you move, how you speak, how you treat people, and how you handle adversity.

Gratitude doesn't make you weak. It makes you steady.

And when you start your day from that place, affirmations stop being wishful thinking and start becoming alignment. You're not trying to convince yourself of something that isn't true. You're declaring the direction you're walking, grounded in what's already real.

If you did nothing else but start each morning naming what you're grateful for, your life would change. Not because circumstances magically improve overnight, but because you finally see clearly how much grace is already present.

Gratitude sharpens your vision.

And once you see clearly, you move differently.

> **"He is a wise man who does not grieve for the things which he has not, but rejoices for those which he has."**
> —Epictetus

DAY 20 TASK: START WITH GRATITUDE

1. **Write down five things you are grateful for today.** Keep them real. Breath. Health. A second chance. People who support you. Work that matters. Don't rush this.
2. **Say them out loud first thing in the morning.** Before affirmations. Before planning. Before asking for anything. Let each one land in your body.
3. **Move through the day from this posture.** Notice how you speak, how you respond, how you handle stress. Gratitude is not passive. It's a way of carrying yourself.

Then journal this sentence:

> **"Today, I recognized how much I have already been given."**

Say it again tomorrow.

And the next day.

Until gratitude becomes your baseline, not your backup plan.

CHAPTER 21

YOUR BODY IS A TEMPLE

> **"It is a shame for a man to grow old without seeing the beauty and strength of which his body is capable."**
> —Socrates

In Chapter 20, you learned the importance of gratitude. But if you're going to build a life of strength and purpose, it starts with the one thing you carry through it all: **your body.**

Your body isn't just a machine. It's not some disposable vehicle meant to be run into the ground and replaced.

It's a **sacred vessel.**

The foundation of your power.

The home of your spirit.

The one thing you will carry with you every second of your life.

Yet, the modern world has convinced men to ignore their bodies.

Eat whatever you want.

Drink until you black out.

Sit all day. Never move. Never challenge yourself.

And then they wonder…

Why do I feel weak?

Why is my mind foggy?

Why don't I feel connected to anything anymore?

It's simple.

If you don't take care of your body, **you have nothing.**

Your body is the foundation of your mind.

Your mind is the foundation of your spirit.

A weak body leads to a weak mind, and a weak mind leads to a weak soul.

The entire system collapses.

Discipline over your body isn't just about strength.

It's about **spiritual alignment.**

THE ANCIENT TRUTH: YOUR BODY IS SACRED

This isn't new.

> **"Do you not know that your bodies are temples of the Holy Spirit…? You are not your own; you were bought at a price. Therefore, honor God with your bodies."**
> —1 Corinthians 6:19-20

Your body isn't yours to destroy.

It's a temple. A gift.

It was never meant to be poisoned, numbed, or neglected.

> **"Offer your bodies as a living sacrifice, holy and pleasing to God; this is your true and proper worship."**
> —Romans 12:1

Every workout. Every clean meal. Every cold plunge. Every deep breath.

That's worship.

This is about more than abs.

This is about reverence.

THE PHILOSOPHERS KNEW IT TOO

> **"No man has the right to be an amateur in the matter of physical training... It is a shame for a man to grow old without seeing the beauty and strength of which his body is capable."**
> —Socrates
>
> **"To keep the body in good health is a duty... otherwise, we shall not be able to keep our mind strong and clear."**
> —Buddha
>
> **"A sedentary life is the real sin against the Holy Spirit."**
> —Nietzsche

These men weren't just talking about fitness.

They were talking about **respect.**

They were talking about the body as **the foundation of thought, discipline, and power.**

You ignore it? You lose everything else.

FROM STRENGTH TO MASTERY—MY OWN EVOLUTION

I've always been drawn to strength.

Martial arts. Lifting. Combat. Pushing my body to its absolute limit.

And for a long time, that gave me power.

But it was rooted in **ego.**

I wanted to dominate.

To win.

To be the strongest man in the room.

Now?

I train for life. For longevity. For mastery.

I still train like a warrior, but now I do it like a monk.

Not to prove anything.

But to honor the gift I've been given.

My body is no longer just a weapon.

It's a temple.

HOW TO HONOR YOUR BODY LIKE A WARRIOR

Treating your body like a temple doesn't mean pampering it.

It means respecting it.

- **Train as if your life depends on it, because it does.** Lift. Move. Stretch. Fight. Sweat daily.
- **Fuel like a king, not an enslaved person.** Eat real food. Cut the garbage. Prioritize strength, not comfort.
- **Recover like a professional.** Sleep. Breathe. Meditate. Cold plunges. Ice. Stillness. Nature.

Discipline isn't punishment.

Discipline is **worship.**

FINAL THOUGHT: THE TEMPLE IS THE FIRST BATTLEFIELD

If your body is weak, your discipline is weak.

If your discipline is weak, your mind is weak.

And if your mind is weak, the enemy wins without ever needing to fight.

The world needs stronger men.

Not just on the outside. But in spirit. In presence. In alignment.

Your temple is waiting.

DAY 21 TASK: BUILD YOUR TEMPLE

For the next **seven days**, commit to this challenge:

- Move your body **every single day.** Even if it's just a walk or a stretch.
- Eat **100% clean.** No alcohol. No junk. No poison.
- Prioritize **recovery.** Get seven or more hours of sleep. Avoid screens before bed. Do breathwork.
- Hydrate like a warrior. Fuel with purpose.
- Write this mantra in your journal: **"My body is not a machine. It is a temple. I honor it through discipline."**

Then live it.

Because the man who builds his body…

Builds his life.

CHAPTER 22

TUNING INTO THE FREQUENCY OF LIFE

You've built the temple. You've begun honoring your body as the foundation of everything. Now it's time to go deeper into the energy that animates it all.

I've always been fascinated by energy, the kind you can't see but can feel.

The moment you walk into a room and **just know** something's off.

The way certain people drain you… and others lift you.

The way music, words, and even a passing thought can shift your entire emotional state.

For a long time, I thought this was just intuition.

But the deeper I explored, the more I realized,

Everything operates on a frequency.

Not just people.

Everything.

The whole world runs on energy.

The question is:

What station are you tuned into?

EVERYTHING IS ENERGY

> **"Everything in life is vibration."**
> —Albert Einstein

Science has finally caught up to what ancient wisdom has said for centuries:

Everything is vibrating.

The chair you're sitting in.

The food you eat.

Your thoughts.

Your emotions.

Even your body.

It's all energy.

Just moving at different speeds.

- High frequencies: **love, gratitude, joy.**
- Low frequencies: **fear, anger, resentment.**

Just like a radio, you are constantly tuning into signals, most of the time **without even realizing it.**

And what happens when millions of people are tuned into the same low station?

THE COLLECTIVE FREQUENCY—HOW WE SHAPE THE WORLD

Imagine human consciousness like one massive ocean.

Each of us is a drop.

And every thought, emotion, or action we send out?

It ripples.

When the collective frequency is high:

You see unity, love, purpose, and creation.

But when the frequency drops?

You see war.

Division.

Anxiety.

Addiction.

A world addicted to low vibrations.

You think it's a coincidence that the news runs on fear?

That social media thrive on outrage?

That we're constantly being bombarded with reasons to be angry, scared, or numb?

It's not.

Because fear is a low frequency.

And a population vibrating at fear…

is easier to control.

TUNING YOUR OWN FREQUENCY

Here's the truth:

You don't need to change the entire ocean.

But you can change **your drop.**

Raising your frequency isn't about being delusional or blind to what's wrong.

It's about choosing to **rise above it.**

- You tune into **gratitude** and feel the lift.
- You turn off the noise and feel the clarity.
- You spend time with people who elevate you and make you feel **lighter.**

Your frequency affects everyone around you.

Energy is contagious.

> "Those who are awake live in a state of
> constant amazement."
> —Buddha

THE FREQUENCIES OF GOD AND THE DEVIL

This ties back to the central message of the book:

We Are All God. We Are All the Devil.

- God is the **highest frequency**: love, presence, creation.
- The Devil is the **lowest**: fear, destruction, separation.

Every moment, you choose who you're aligning with.

Ask yourself:

- Am I contracting or expanding?
- Am I lifting, or pulling down?
- Am I reacting out of fear or creating out of love?

The world shifts when men choose higher frequencies.

Not just for themselves.

But for the collective.

BREAKING FREE FROM THE LOW FREQUENCIES OF THE WORLD

The system is designed to keep you stuck.

Fear-based headlines.

Consumer culture.

Distraction disguised as entertainment.

All of it is noise.

All of it is static.

All of it keeps you vibrating at a **low level.**

But once you **see it**, you can't unsee it.

And once you **choose differently**, the world starts responding.

You begin to protect your energy.

You stop engaging in drama.

You align with people, places, and practices that help you rise.

And suddenly…

Life feels lighter.

You feel more like yourself.

THE POWER OF ONE SHIFT

You don't need to be a guru.

You don't need a million followers.

You don't need the whole world to get it.

You just need to shift your own frequency.

Because when **one man rises**, others feel it.

One clear voice cuts through the static.

One loving presence calms chaos.

One man vibrating higher can shift an entire room.

So ask yourself:

What station am I tuned into?

And who do I become when I change the dial?

DAY 22 TASK: TUNE IN AND ELEVATE

Today, protect your frequency like it's your greatest asset, because it is.

- **Turn off one low-frequency input.** That might be the news, social media, gossip, or junk TV.
- **Spend 10 minutes** in silence or with high-frequency music, breathing, visualizing, or just feeling.
- **Write down your "tuning mantra."** *"I choose to tune into love, strength, and presence. I raise the frequency everywhere I go."*
- **Bonus:** Take a walk in nature. Let the earth help you recalibrate.

Your frequency is your power.

Rise with it.

CHAPTER 23

THE POWER OF YOUR ENVIRONMENT

CREATING HEAVEN OR HELL AROUND YOU

You've tuned into your frequency. Now ask yourself: What kind of environment are you broadcasting it into?

Because what I believe is that:

> You can have the strongest mindset, the clearest goals, the deepest faith, but if your environment is working against you, **you're trying to grow roots in concrete.**

Your environment is either pulling you toward **heaven.**

or dragging you back into **hell.**

There is no neutral.

THE LIE OF WILLPOWER

Most men overestimate willpower and underestimate the environment.

They try to grind through toxic workplaces.

They stay in relationships that drain them.

They sleep in cluttered rooms, scroll through negativity, and wonder why they feel like shit every morning.

And then they beat themselves up for not being stronger.

But here's the truth:

Your environment is shaping you more than your discipline ever will.

You don't just live in your environment.

It lives in you.

If you want to rise, you need to design a world that helps you rise.

WHY I MOVED TO COSTA RICA

I didn't move to Costa Rica for a vacation.

I moved because I was suffocating in my old life.

Too much noise. Too much chaos. Too much static.

Then I came to Nosara.

I stepped outside.

Felt the sun on my skin.

Heard the ocean.

I breathed deeply for what felt like the first time in years.

Something shifted.

And it wasn't just the environment.

It was **me**, responding to it.

That's when I realized:

Your location carries a vibration.

Some places drain you.

Some places wake you the hell up.

And it wasn't just me.

I met people from all over the world who had felt the same pull.

They weren't escaping life.

They were remembering it.

But you don't have to move across the world to change your environment.

You just must get intentional.

HOW TO BUILD HEAVEN—WHEREVER YOU ARE

1. Upgrade Your Physical Space

- **Declutter.** Chaos around you creates chaos within you.
- **Bring in nature.** Plants. Fresh air. Open windows. Light.
- **Make it sacred.** Your home is your temple. Treat it like one.

Ask yourself: Does this space reflect the man I'm becoming?

2. Audit Your Relationships

- Do your friends **challenge and elevate** you?
- Or do they keep you stuck in the same old story?
- Do your conversations inspire action, or do they just consist of complaining about everything?

This isn't about cutting everyone off.

It's about **choosing your circle like your life depends on it.**

Because it does.

3. Control What You Consume

Your mental environment matters just as much.

- What are you watching?
- What are you listening to?
- Are you scrolling your life away or feeding your fire?

Your attention is your energy.

Protect it like your future depends on it, **because it does.**

4. Spend More Time in Nature

Nature is the original high-frequency environment.

It grounds you. Clears your mind. It resets your nervous system.

Can't move to the jungle?

Cool.

Find your version of it.

- A park.
- A trail.

- A quiet balcony in the morning sun.
- A walk under the stars.

You don't need paradise.

You just need to create it in your day.

YOU ARE THE ARCHITECT

Your environment is either building you…

or breaking you.

You don't have to accept it the way it is.

You don't have to live in noise, clutter, drama, and distraction.

You can choose.

You can shift.

You can create a life that **pulls you forward** instead of constantly dragging you back.

Heaven is not a place.

It's a **state of being.**

And the easiest way to step into it?

Build your environment to match your highest self.

DAY 23 TASK: AUDIT YOUR ENVIRONMENT

Today, do a full check-in.

- **Look around your space.** What needs to go? What needs to be added?
- **Look at your relationships.** Who drains you? Who fuels you?
- **Look at your inputs.** What are you consuming, watching, listening to? Write this in your journal and finish the sentence: *"If my environment matched the man I'm becoming, it would look like…"* Then pick **one** change and do it **today.**

You are not stuck.

You are the architect.

CHAPTER 24

THE PLACES THAT CALL US

> "He who would live in peace must choose his environment carefully."
> —Confucius

Some places you choose.

Some places choose you.

I didn't just move to Nosara.

Nosara moved me.

From the outside, it looks like a sleepy surf town; jungle roads, yoga classes, world-class waves.

But if you know, you know.

There's something else here.

A current you can't see, but you can feel.

This place pulls people in.

Not tourists. Not wanderers.

Seekers. Healers. Builders. Warriors.

People who are waking up.

People who are on the edge of transformation, whether they know it or not.

And once you arrive, something inside of you says,

"This is it."

THE GLITCH IN THE MATRIX

I had a moment recently that made all of this even more real.

I was talking to someone about this book; how it's been unfolding, how AI is playing a role, how aligned everything feels.

A little while later, I'm having a totally separate conversation with a couple and their five-month-old baby. It's one of those talks that starts as small talk and then suddenly dives deep, as they often do here.

Then the guy from my earlier conversation walks up and asks how to build a GPT.

Before I can respond, the woman with the baby speaks up.

"Oh, I actually helped create ChatGPT."

I stopped.

"Wait, what?"

"Yeah," she said. "I was one of the original designers. One of the three who built it."

There was no way that was just chance.

I had been speaking this book into existence…

And the universe sent me the woman who literally built the tool helping me write it.

That's when I knew:

Nosara isn't random. It's orchestrated.

CERTAIN PLACES CARRY POWER

Nosara isn't alone.

There are other places like it.

- Sedona.
- Bali.
- Machu Picchu.
- Glastonbury.

Places that hum with something ancient.

Places that seem to **pull** people in when they're ready to level up.

Some say it's energy lines, ley lines pulsing through the Earth.

Some say it's the spiritual residue of centuries of prayer, ritual, and healing.

I don't pretend to know for sure.

But I do know this:

THE RIGHT PLACE CAN CHANGE YOUR LIFE.

Because when you're in the right place,

you remember who you really are.

SAYING YES TO THE PULL

I could've ignored the pull.

Stayed in Tennessee. Played it safe.

Kept doing what I knew.

But I listened.

And since then?

The right people keep showing up.

The right moments keep unfolding.

The signs are too clear to ignore.

Because when you say yes to the unknown,

life meets you halfway.

It's like the universe has been waiting for you to stop hesitating.

And once you do, it says:

> "Good. Now watch what happens next."

> Nosara as a Mirror

Nosara didn't just give me peace.

It gave me a mirror.

It showed me where I was still hiding.

It pushed me toward my purpose.

It stripped away what wasn't real.

This place doesn't let you coast.

It invites you to become.

To step fully into the man you're meant to be.

That's why this book is being written here.

It couldn't have been born anywhere else.

THE VORTEX IS INSIDE YOU

Here's the part most people miss:

Nosara didn't *give* me my power.

It reminded me I had it all along.

The real vortex isn't out there.

It's **in you.**

That energy that pulls you toward certain places, people, and experiences?

It's your own inner guidance finally getting loud enough to hear.

And when you trust it?

You stop chasing.

Because the right things start finding you.

> **"First we shape our environments, then our environments shape us."**
> —Winston Churchill

FINAL THOUGHT: TRUST THE PULL

If a place keeps showing up in your dreams…

If a city name keeps popping into your life…

If your gut whispers, "Go…" even if it doesn't make sense.

Listen.

Because some places aren't just places.

They're portals.

And if you trust the call,

they'll take you exactly where you're meant to be.

DAY 24 TASK: LISTEN FOR THE PLACE

Today, take 10 quiet minutes.

Ask yourself:

- Is there a place I've always felt drawn to?
- Where do I feel most alive, most myself?
- Is there somewhere I've been resisting, even though I feel pulled?

Write it down.

Even if you don't know why.

Then take one small action:

Look it up. Book a flight. Plan a visit.

Say yes to the pull.

And let the rest unfold.

CHAPTER 25

THE POWER OF OWNING YOUR MORNING

> **"Well begun is half done."**
> —Aristotle

How you start your day determines how you live your life.

Most people don't realize it, but the moment they open their eyes, they're already making a choice.

A choice to lead, or to follow.

To set the tone, or to let the world set it for them.

And most people?

They choose wrong.

They hit snooze.

They scroll their phones.

They invite noise, chaos, and distraction into their minds before they've even taken a breath.

By the time they're out the door, they've already lost the day.

Because if you start in chaos, your day will be chaotic.

If you start in weakness, your day will be weak.

But if you start in **discipline, stillness, and power,** then the world moves around you, not through you.

THE MORNING RITUAL FOR MASTERY

A warrior doesn't step into battle without a ritual.

And every morning, like it or not, you step into battle.

If you wake up and **react**, you're already behind.

But if you wake up and **choose**, you start the day already winning.

Here's how you take control:

1. Breathwork & Meditation: Start in Stillness

Before the world gets a chance to speak, you speak to yourself.

Close your eyes. Breathe with intention.

Silence the noise before it starts.

You don't need an hour. You need **presence**.

Stillness in the morning creates power for the rest of the day.

2. Movement—Wake the Body to Wake the Mind

You were not made to stay still.

A few minutes of stretching. A short workout. A walk in silence.

You don't need a gym. You need movement.

Motion is medicine.

Energy is not something you wait for. It's something you **generate**.

3. Affirmations—Program Your Mind

Words create reality.

So what are you saying to yourself every morning?

Instead of repeating old doubts and fears, speak power into your day.

"I am focused."

"I am clear."

"I am strong."

"I am building something meaningful."

Say it like you mean it.

Because your mind is listening.

4. Learn Something—Feed Your Mind First

Most people start the day consuming garbage.

News. Notifications. Fear.

Choose wisdom instead.

Read something that sharpens you.

Listen to something that lifts you.

Feed your mind with clarity, not chaos.

AHREN AND THE SHIFT AT THE BALANCED MAN RETREAT

When I launched *The Balanced Man Retreat*, I wanted it to be more than a break from life.

I wanted it to be a reset. A recalibration.

But it wasn't until my friend and partner Ahren led a morning practice that everything changed.

He gathered the group at sunrise.

No phones. No noise. Just breath, movement, and intention.

We started with deep breathing to oxygenate the body and clear the mind.

Then, a simple movement to wake the warrior.

Then, affirmations spoken aloud, our voices anchoring truth into our day.

Finally, silence.

Stillness.

The shift was instant.

Men who had arrived anxious and heavy now stood taller.

They moved with clarity.

They spoke with purpose.

They started leading themselves again.

From that day forward, morning ritual became a non-negotiable.

Because when you **own the morning**, you **own the man**.

THE HABIT THAT CHANGES EVERYTHING

This isn't about adding more to your to-do list.

It's about subtracting the things that steal your power.

- No more checking your phone before checking in with yourself.
- No more snoozing on your potential.
- No more starting the day as a slave to distraction.

Instead:

- **Wake with purpose.**
- **Move with power.**
- **Speak with clarity.**
- **Choose yourself.**

Because the truth is simple:

You don't rise to the level of your goals.

You fall to the level of your habits.

And it all starts when the alarm goes off.

> **"If you win the morning, you win the day."**
> —Tim Ferriss

DAY 25 TASK: CREATE YOUR MORNING RITUAL

Tonight, set the stage.

- Prepare your space.
- Leave your phone across the room.
- Write your affirmations.
- Choose one small way to move.
- Set an intention for what you'll learn or read.

Then tomorrow morning: **Execute.**

Don't hit snooze. Don't reach for your phone.

Just start.

Breathe.

Move.

Speak.

Focus.

Master your morning.

Master your life.

CHAPTER 26

THE MANIFESTO

DECLARING WHO YOU ARE

Your words create your reality.

Most people don't realize it, but every day, casting spells on their life, on their future, and on their identity.

They just don't know it.

Because instead of spells of strength, they're casting spells of limitation.

"I'm not good enough."

"I can't do this."

"I always mess things up."

"This is just who I am."

They say these things with casual certainty, not realizing that every time they do, they're building a cage around themselves.

Brick by brick. Word by word.

But here's the truth:

Your words are not just sounds.

They are instructions.

Commands to your subconscious.

Declarations to your soul.

Blueprints for your future.

That's why it's called **"spelling."**

So the question is:

What are you spelling into existence?

THE POWER OF THE MANIFESTO

Most men drift because they've never decided who they are.

They wake up reactive, letting their thoughts, habits, and beliefs run on autopilot.

But imagine waking up every morning and hearing the voice of your highest self.

A voice that reminds you of your power.

Your values.

Your purpose.

Your *truth*.

That's what a **Manifesto** is.

It's not wishful thinking.

It's not fake positivity.

It's a line in the sand.

It's you saying:

This is who I am.

This is how I live.

This is what I'm creating.

And once you speak it, every day, with conviction, your subconscious starts to believe it.

Your thoughts align.

Your actions follow.

And your world begins to shift.

HOW TO CREATE YOUR MANIFESTO

This is your code. Your declaration. Your internal mission statement.

Follow these steps to write it with power:

1. Write it in the present tense.

Not "I want to be."

Not "I will be."

Say: "I *am*."

2. Don't worry about how.

Speak what you believe deep down is possible, even if your current reality doesn't match it yet.

3. Make it powerful.

No fluff. Every word should land like a punch. Mean every sentence.

4. Read it every morning.

Out loud. With fire. With presence. This isn't a whisper, it's a *declaration.*

5. Live by it.

It's not just something you say, it's something you *embody.*

6. Be specific.

Dates. Locations. Results. "My family and I are living in Costa Rica by 2027." Make it real.

7. Sign it.

Put your name at the bottom. Own it. And write:

"My name is [your name], and I always keep my promises."

MY MANIFESTO

About a year ago, I started doing this.

And everything changed.

Here's part of what I say every single morning:

"I am strong.

I am focused.

I am disciplined.

I move with power and purpose.

Every day, I expand in love, abundance, success, and health.

I am a creator of my reality.

I am a warrior.

I am a leader.

I am a man who walks with integrity.

Nothing controls me.

I choose my path, and I walk it with confidence."

This isn't just something I recite.

It's something I *live*.

Also, this is just how I wrote my manifesto. Ahren turned his in to a cool article that was written about him by a writer he likes. You can turn it into a cool podcast using AI tools. It really doesn't matter as long as you read it, listen to it, and believe it. Don't get lost in the how. Feel it with a knowing in your being!

> **"The limits of my language mean the limits of my world."**
> —Ludwig Wittgenstein

THE REALITY SHIFT

If your self-talk is filled with doubt, your life will be filled with hesitation.

If your inner voice is weak, your actions will be weak.

But if your words are powerful, your world will reflect it.

This is not mystical. It's mechanical.

It's psychology. It's repetition. It's *neuroplasticity.*

When you say something with conviction every day, your brain starts building new pathways.

You become the man you declare yourself to be.

Thoughts → Words

Words → Beliefs

Beliefs → Actions

Actions → Results

So ask yourself:

What have I been declaring lately?

Is it leading me toward the man I want to be, or away from him?

FINAL THOUGHT: SPEAK IT INTO EXISTENCE

Every single morning, you face a choice:

Let the world tell you who you are.

Or tell the world who you *decide* to be.

The strongest men I know?

They don't wait for clarity.

They speak it.

They declare it.

They *become* it.

So, take the time today to write your manifesto.

Craft it as if your life depends on it.

Because it does.

Do **NOT** worry about the how!

Read it every morning.

Speak it out loud.

And then back it up with action.

Because when your words match your walk, **you become unstoppable.**

DAY 26 TASK: WRITE YOUR MANIFESTO

Today is about putting it all on paper. Who you are. What you stand for. How you choose to live.

Write your personal manifesto. Not a wish list. Not a dream board. A declaration.

Start with:

- "I am..." (Followed by who you choose to be)
- "I will always..." (your non-negotiables)
- "I will never..." (the lines you won't cross)
- "Every day, I commit to..." (your daily standard)

Keep it short. Clear. Direct. And real.

Sign it with your name at the bottom. This is your promise to yourself. Read it every morning. Speak it like you mean it.

This is who you are now. Live like it.

CHAPTER 27

THE BREATH OF LIFE

A FORGOTTEN PATH TO GOD

> **"The soul is the breath of God."**
> —Gregory of Nazianzus

You've declared who you are.

Now it's time to remember what you are.

Because even with the strongest manifesto, even with daily affirmations and focused discipline, there's one path most men still overlook; a doorway to power that requires no words, no beliefs, no tools.

Only breath.

The most ancient practice on earth.

The most direct line to God.

And the most forgotten.

THE TRUTH HIDDEN IN PLAIN SIGHT

I didn't expect it to change my life.

I had already walked many spiritual paths, including meditation, prayer, and plant medicine. I had chased moments of clarity and glimpses of the divine. But something was still missing. I was always reaching outward.

And then one day, I surrendered to a breathwork session.

No substances. No chants. No expectations. Just deep, rhythmic breathing.

And somewhere in the stillness, it hit me:

> **"You've been looking outside. But the power has been within you all along."**

In that moment, I felt it, not just an idea or a belief, but a visceral, undeniable connection. My breath wasn't just air moving through my lungs. It was a prayer. A bridge. A lifeline back to God.

IN THE BEGINNING WAS BREATH

Genesis says God formed man from dust, but it wasn't until He **breathed** into his nostrils that man became a living soul (Genesis 2:7).

Not the flesh. Not the body. The breath.

The first act of life is an inhale.

The last act before death is an exhale.

Everything in between? Borrowed breath.

Some ancient Hebrew scholars believe the name of God, YHWH, was never meant to be spoken, but **breathed**.

Inhale: Yah

Exhale: Weh

What if every breath you've ever taken has been whispering God's name?

What if even in your darkest moments, even in sin, shame, or suffering, you were still in communion with the divine?

You just forgot to listen.

THE FORGOTTEN WEAPON

If breath is so powerful, why doesn't anyone teach us how to use it?

Simple:

Because a man connected to his breath is a man who **can't be controlled**.

He doesn't need a pill to manage his stress.

He doesn't need to escape through alcohol, porn, or distraction.

He doesn't need to be told who he is, because he already knows.

And men like that?

They're dangerous.

To systems built on fear.

To businesses built on addiction.

To religions built on dependence.

So we're taught to look elsewhere.

To seek peace outside of ourselves.

To chase God instead of breathing Him in.

But you don't have to chase what's already inside you.

BREATHWORK IS THE BRIDGE

> **"Breath is the bridge which connects life
> to consciousness, which unites your
> body to your thoughts."**
> —Thích Nhất Hạnh

Holotropic breathwork changed everything for me.

Not because it gave me something new, but because it stripped away what wasn't true.

It revealed the parts of me I was hiding from.

It cleared emotional baggage I didn't know I was carrying.

It gave me access to clarity, peace, and presence I had been searching for elsewhere.

No psychedelics.

No guru.

Just breath.

It was like plant medicine, but without the plants.

A spiritual experience with nothing but oxygen and presence.

Because **breath is the bridge** between body and spirit, between ego and soul, between man and God.

I have taught fighting and self-defense for 30 years, and I love it. However, I was always teaching people a skill I hoped they would never have to use in real life. Now I also teach holotropic breathwork, and I hope people practice on some level every day.

THE G-BREATH—POWER IN PRACTICE

At The Balanced Man Retreat, we start every day with activation.

We don't reach for our phones. We don't stumble into the day half-awake.

We breathe with intention. We breathe with power.

Thanks to my brother, Jeremy Jackson, we now use a breathwork protocol we call the **"G-Breath."**

This isn't soft breathwork for relaxation.

It's breathwork for warriors. For men who are ready to flip the switch.

One full round includes:

1. Inhale through the mouth, exhale through the mouth.
2. Inhale through the mouth, exhale through the nose.
3. Inhale through the nose, exhale through the nose.
4. Inhale through the nose, exhale through the mouth.

That's one round.

Do it 13 times.

No breaks. No distractions. Just rhythm and power.

By the end, you're buzzing.

Grounded. Alive. Focused.

Ready to lead instead of reacting.

WHY EVERY MAN NEEDS TO BREATHE LIKE THIS

Because most men are breathing just enough to stay alive, not enough to **feel alive**.

You want clarity? Breathe.

You want strength? Breathe.

You want to stop feeling anxious, lost, or weak?

Learn to master your breath.

Because a man who controls his breath controls his mind.

And a man who controls his mind controls his reality.

FINAL THOUGHT: GOD IS CLOSER THAN YOU THINK

Maybe you don't need to find God.

Maybe you just need to slow down long enough to feel Him and let Him find you.

He's not hiding.

He's not distant.

He's not waiting for you to become perfect.

He's in every inhale.

He's in every exhale.

And when the noise of the world fades, and all that's left is breath, you'll hear the truth that's been there all along:

You are not alone.

You never have been.

DAY 27 TASK: THE 13-ROUND
G-BREATH CHALLENGE

Tomorrow morning, before you do anything else:

1. Sit or stand in a quiet place with a straight spine.
2. Complete **13 full rounds** of the G-Breath:
   - Inhale through the mouth, exhale through the mouth
   - Inhale through the mouth, exhale through the nose
   - Inhale through the nose, exhale through the nose
   - Inhale through the nose, exhale through the mouth
3. After the last round, sit in silence for one minute. Breathe normally. Let your body settle. Listen.

Then ask yourself:

- What do I feel?
- What do I hear?
- What do I now know?

This is the beginning of your return.

You've spoken your manifesto.

Now breathe it into existence.

CHAPTER 28

PLANT MEDICINE

A TOOL FOR LIBERATION OR A THREAT TO CONTROL?

We've talked about breath, our direct line to presence, power, and God. It's a tool that's been with us from the moment we arrived. But breath isn't the only forgotten tool we've been given. There are others. Older. Wilder. Misunderstood. And for many, feared.

Because what happens when you remember who you are, without anyone else telling you?

I remember the first time I took psilocybin with intention.

Not to party.

Not to escape.

But to meet myself.

It wasn't a loud experience. There was no chaos, no loss of control, no hallucinated dragons or fireworks. Just presence. Deep, overwhelming presence. The feeling that I wasn't alone, not in my mind, not in my body, and certainly not in this world.

I felt connected to God more than I ever had sitting in a church pew.

No pastor. No choir. No doctrine.

Just silence, nature, breath… and something else.

Something divine.

And that's when the question landed in my gut:

If this is healing… if this is connection… if this is clarity… then why is it feared?

Why is it banned?

Are these medicines dangerous?

Or are they just dangerous to the systems that feed off our disconnection?

> **"The psychotic drowns in the same waters**
> **in which the mystic swims with delight."**
> —Joseph Campbell

A TOOL OR A WEAPON? THE POWER OF INTENTION

Like anything powerful, plant medicine can liberate or destroy.

It's not the tool. It's the intention.

Fire can cook your food or burn down your house.

A knife can feed your family or end a life.

Water can cleanse or drown.

Plant medicine is no different.

I've seen men crack open under ayahuasca and release grief they'd been holding for decades. I've seen women reconnect with their inner child after years of trauma. I've seen people finally forgive themselves and feel peace.

But I've also seen misuse.

I've seen people chase the high without doing the work. Turn sacred experiences into party favors. Use it as an escape instead of transformation.

Same medicine. Different outcome.

And that's the part most people don't talk about.

It's not about what you take.

It's about *why* you take it.

Why Is It Really Illegal?

Let's be honest.

This isn't about safety.

If it were, alcohol wouldn't be sold on every corner.

Tobacco wouldn't be advertised with smiling faces.

Pharmaceutical companies wouldn't be profiting off pills that kill more people every year than all psychedelics combined.

So why is psilocybin, a mushroom that grows from the ground, considered a Schedule I drug?

Why is ayahuasca, a jungle brew used for centuries by indigenous healers, considered more dangerous than the very substances destroying lives daily?

Because plant medicine doesn't make people obedient.

It doesn't keep them numb, distracted, or addicted.

It wakes them up.

And a population that wakes up?

That remembers their sovereignty?

That questions the system?

That's a threat.

THE RELIGION OF CONTROL

Even in spiritual communities, plant medicine is taboo.

Too risky. Too weird. Too "new age."

But let's rewind.

Moses went into the wilderness and came back with clarity.

Jesus fasted for 40 days before stepping into his mission.

Mystics across traditions have used solitude, altered states, and ritual to access the divine.

And yet, the moment someone uses plant medicine to connect to that same divinity, they're called reckless. Or worse, demonic.

But what if the danger isn't that these tools lead us away from God…

What if they lead us *directly to Him*, with no go-between required?

That's the real fear.

RESPECT THE PATH

This chapter is not a permission slip.

Plant medicine is not a shortcut. It's not a replacement for work, prayer, stillness, breath, or integration. It's not a quick fix or a spiritual hack.

It's a mirror.

And mirrors don't lie.

If you choose this path, walk it with reverence.

Set. Setting. Intention. Guidance. Integration.

If those five words don't mean anything to you, you're not ready.

But if they do, if you're willing to face what you see in that mirror, then know this:

It can change everything.

I would also like to say that, during a plant medicine ceremony, I was shown that not all mushrooms and vines, like ayahuasca, are "good" or have the highest frequency. If you think about the nature of a vine, especially, and other plants that come from the ground, it wraps around you and wants to keep you here on Earth. So, if you are going to do plant medicine, please make sure you know the source of the plants, the Shaman, the other people at the ceremony, and most importantly, perhaps, your intention and purpose behind doing it in the first place.

WAKING UP ISN'T ALWAYS COMFORTABLE

> **"The privilege of a lifetime is to become**
> **who you truly are."**
> —Carl Jung

Plant medicine doesn't give you answers. It reveals what's already there.

And what's there might not be pretty.

But if you're willing to see it… you can finally choose something different.

DAY 28 TASK: RECLAIM THE QUESTION

Whether or not you ever use plant medicine is irrelevant.

This is about **agency**.

About **awakening**.

About **truth**.

Today, ask yourself:

- Where in my life have I been outsourcing my healing?
- What tools have I been taught to fear?
- What parts of myself am I still avoiding?

And then write down one thing you've judged without fully understanding.

It could be plant medicine. It could be meditation. It could be silence.

Now research it. Sit with it. Question the story you've been given.

Because freedom begins when you stop letting other people define what's true for you.

You are your own permission slip.

The medicine is already inside you.

All tools do is **remind you.**

CHAPTER 29

TECHNOLOGY

A TOOL OR A TRAP?

Plant medicine may offer us a key to remembering who we are, but not everyone is called to that path. The truth is, you don't have to travel to the jungle or enter an altered state to wake up. Sometimes the challenge isn't accessing ancient wisdom. It's surviving the modern world.

And nothing defines that modern world more than this: **technology.**

Technology has given us power beyond anything our ancestors could have imagined.

We can communicate across the world in seconds. We can access the knowledge of entire civilizations with a few taps on a screen. We can use artificial intelligence to enhance our lives, automate tasks, and unlock new levels of creativity.

Heck, I wouldn't have written this book without AI.

But for all its power, technology comes with a cost.

It can connect us or isolate us.

It can inform us or manipulate us.

It can make us stronger or enslave us.

The real question isn't whether technology is good or bad.

It's whether you control it, or it controls you.

> **"Men have become the tools of their tools."**
> —Henry David Thoreau

THE ILLUSION OF CONNECTION

We've never been more "connected."

And we've never felt more alone.

You can FaceTime someone in another time zone.

You can get likes from people you haven't seen in a decade.

You can post updates that make you look "happy" while you're silently drowning.

We've replaced *presence* with performance.

Intimacy with interaction.

Truth with highlight reels.

We used to sit around fires, tell stories, challenge each other, and sharpen each other.

Now? We scroll. We lurk. We compare.

The screen was meant to connect us, but more often than not, it's become a wall.

Technology is not the enemy.

Mindless consumption is.

SOCIAL MEDIA: MIRROR OR MIRAGE?

Social media was built to connect us.

But it's optimized to control us.

Every feature, the infinite scroll, the notifications, the likes, is engineered to keep you on the platform. Not to empower you. To *monetize* your attention.

And here's the punch in the gut:

Most men are *watching* other men live.

They follow fitness influencers instead of training.

They watch millionaires instead of building something.

They repost motivational quotes instead of doing the work.

They consume. And consume. And consume.

And then wonder why they feel powerless.

But think about this:

What if you *created* instead of consumed?

What if you *posted* instead of scrolled?

What if you *built* instead of watched?

Social media isn't the problem.

A lack of purpose is.

THE DEATH OF PRESENCE

We've lost the art of being **with** people.

We send emojis instead of making eye contact.

We text when we should talk.

We skim when we should listen.

It's not just about communication. It's about **connection**.

Presence is a muscle. And most men have let it atrophy.

If you can't sit with someone and speak truthfully, if you rely on a phone to say what you really feel, if you avoid real conversations because they feel "too intense," you're not in control. You're hiding.

A strong man values presence.

He doesn't need a screen to be seen.

AI: AMPLIFIER OR REPLACEMENT?

Artificial intelligence is the most powerful tool mankind has ever created.

It can speed up your thinking, help you problem-solve, and unlock new levels of creativity.

Or...

It can replace your thinking entirely.

The moment you stop using your mind because a machine can do it faster, you're not using AI; you're *losing* yourself.

AI should *amplify* your power, not replace it.

It should buy you time to build deeper things, not make you lazy.

Like any tool, it reflects the man who wields it.

Use it with vision? It will make you unstoppable.

Use it without intention? It will make you irrelevant.

THE STRONG MAN MASTERS HIS TOOLS

The weak man is a slave to technology.

He wakes up and checks his phone before he even checks in with himself.

He scrolls for hours, consumes garbage, and lets algorithms tell him what to think.

He's plugged in, but disconnected from his power.

The strong man?

He controls his inputs.

- He uses social media for growth, not distraction.
- He texts with purpose, but seeks real conversation.
- He leverages AI, but still sharpens his mind.

The strong man doesn't reject technology.

He just refuses to be ruled by it.

Because tools don't make you strong.

How you use them does.

FROM TOOLS TO TRUTH

Mastering your environment isn't about escaping the world.

It's about shaping it, one decision at a time.

And nowhere is that more important than in your relationship with technology.

Because what you consume, you become.

And what you allow into your space will shape the man you are becoming.

DAY 29 TASK: TAKE BACK CONTROL

Today, do an honest audit of your digital life.

- How many hours did you spend on your phone yesterday?
- What apps are dominating your attention?
- Are you consuming more than you're creating?
- When was the last time you had a deep, face-to-face conversation?

Now, set boundaries.

- **Unfollow** accounts that don't challenge or inspire you.
- **Turn off** non-essential notifications.
- **Schedule** 30 minutes to write, create, or build something today with no distractions.
- **Call** someone instead of texting them.

Technology is not your enemy.

Distraction is.

Choose creation. Choose presence. Choose discipline.

Because a man who can inputs can control his life.

CHAPTER 30

THE FINAL GROUNDING

HOW TO APPLY ALL OF THIS

We've looked to the skies for answers. We've questioned history, tradition, science, and even the fabric of reality itself. But the ultimate truth isn't found in ancient ruins or distant galaxies. It's found in the choices you make, right here, right now. This chapter isn't about new ideas. It's about action. Because knowing the path is meaningless if you don't walk it.

This book was never meant to be just read.

It's not a collection of motivational quotes or a feel-good spiritual journey to forget by next week.

Every chapter, every insight, every uncomfortable truth was a doorway, an invitation to wake the hell up and **take control of your life**.

Because knowledge without action is weakness.

The world wants you asleep. Distracted. Numb.

It wants you to be obedient, to scroll instead of build, to consume instead of create, to survive instead of lead.

But now you've seen the truth.

Now you know the game.

And the only way to win is to **refuse to play by their rules**.

YOU ARE THE ARCHITECT NOW

You don't need more motivation.

You need **ownership**.

Own your time.

Own your thoughts.

Own your patterns.

Own your fucking life.

Everything this book has pointed toward comes down to this one truth:

You are in control.

Of your mind.

Of your body.

Of your path.

The only thing standing between the man you are and the man you could become is the choice to step into that power, **daily**.

THE PROOF IS IN THE PATTERN

This isn't woo-woo. This isn't guesswork.

Science is catching up to what the mystics have always known:

Your **consciousness** shapes reality.

My friend Glenn introduced me to something that blew that truth wide open: **Euler's Identity**.

A mathematical equation so beautiful, so precise, that many scientists call it proof of divine structure.

$$e^{\wedge}i\pi + 1 = 0$$

It weaves together energy (e), the unseen (i), the infinite cycle (π), and the mystery of everything and nothing (1 and 0).

It's not just math, it's a **map**. A cosmic signature of creation.

And guess what?

Your thoughts follow the same formula.

Imagination + emotion + focus = manifestation.

What you believe becomes your lens.

What you focus on becomes your frequency.

What you repeat becomes your reality.

THE WORK GLENN AND IVS ARE DOING

Glenn didn't just talk about this stuff; he lived it. He backed it. He poured time, money, and energy into the **Institute for Venture Science** (IVS), founded by Dr. Gerald Pollack and Dr. Jim Ryder.

This isn't some conspiracy lab.

This is where science goes to be **free**, uncontrolled by politics, profit, or outdated paradigms.

IVS funds research that most universities are too scared to touch:

- What if **thoughts shape matter**?
- What if **consciousness is the fundamental force** of the universe?
- What if science and spirituality were never separate to begin with?

These are the questions that **matter**.

And now, you know why.

THE 10 PILLARS TO STAY AWAKE AND IN POWER

Reading this book changed nothing.

Living it will change everything.

Here's your blueprint:

1. **Master Your Mornings.** Win the first hour, win the day. Breathwork. Movement. Mindset. Non-negotiable.
2. **Protect Your Environment.** Toxic people. Weak conversations. Dead energy. Clear it out. Surround yourself with power.
3. **Train Your Body Relentlessly.** Your physical strength is your spiritual foundation. No strength = no discipline = no clarity.
4. **Own Your Mind.** Stop letting your thoughts run you. Program them. Guard them. Speak with power.
5. **Do the Hard Shit Daily.** Cold. Challenge. Reps. Struggle. Pain. That's where growth lives. Comfort is decay.
6. **Stay Connected to Source.** God. Spirit. Consciousness. Call it what you want, **you're not alone.** Tune in.
7. **Build Brotherhood.** Weak men isolate. Strong men unite. Find your tribe. Or stay small.

8. **Be a Creator**. Write. Build. Move. Speak. Don't just scroll and consume. **Put your fingerprint on this world**.
9. **Take Radical Responsibility**. No more excuses. Everything is your fault. That's where your freedom begins.
10. **Walk the Path Every Day.** This isn't a phase. It's not a weekend retreat. It's a way of life.

IT'S NEVER TOO LATE TO BEGIN

If there's one thing I hope you walk away with, it's this:

It is never too late.

Never too late to change.

Never too late to choose differently.

Never too late to rise, reclaim your power, and live the life you were designed for.

I don't care how long you've felt stuck, how far you think you've fallen, or how many chances you believe you've wasted; none of that disqualifies you.

The power we've talked about in this book, the God-given ability to create, to transform, to lead, still lives in you.

Whether you're reading this at at 17 or 77, whether you're just starting your path or finding your way back… the invitation is the same: step in now.

This book hasn't been about perfection.

It's been about permission.

Permission to start.

Permission to stumble.

Permission to become the man you were always meant to be.

Right now, in this moment, you can choose to begin.

> **"No man is free who is not master of himself."**
> —Epictetus

WHY I WROTE THIS BOOK

Because I believe "Big G" **God** wants the best for all of us. I believe he gave us free will to make our lives worth living.

Because I was tired of seeing strong men live like slaves.

Because I've been both the warrior and the coward.

Because I know what it feels like to forget your own power, and what it takes to reclaim it.

I wrote this for the man who knows something's missing.

For the man who's ready to evolve.

For the man who refuses to die asleep.

FINAL THOUGHT: GOD OR DEVIL; YOU DECIDE

You are the creator.

You are the destroyer.

You are the storm and the stillness.

The world wants you weak.

The system wants you numb.

But what I believe?

YOU ARE NOT HERE TO LIVE BY DEFAULT. YOU ARE HERE TO BUILD SOMETHING SACRED.

You don't need another book.

You don't need another teacher.

You don't need permission.

You know what to do.

You know where you've been lying to yourself.

You know where you've been weak.

You know what you've been avoiding.

And you also know what kind of man you're capable of being.

This book didn't give you power.

It reminded you that you already had it.

From here on out, there's no confusion.

Only choice.

Every morning, you decide.

Every action, you choose.

Every excuse, you either keep or burn.

No one is coming to save you.

And that's the best news you'll ever hear.

Because the moment you stop waiting, the moment you take full responsibility, the moment you live what you now know to be true, everything changes.

DAY 30 TASK: YOUR PERSONAL CODE

Today, write your own code.

Not a list of goals. Not resolutions.

Write your **rules for living**, your personal manifesto.

Your commandments. Your non-negotiables.

Start with this prompt:

>"As a man of power, I will always…"

>"I will never…"

>"Every day, I commit to…"

Write 5 to 10. Post them. Read them daily.

Let this be the beginning of a new operating system.

Because this chapter isn't the end.

It's the ignition.

Light it up.

ABOUT THE AUTHOR

Terry Bullman is an entrepreneur, former professional fighter, retreat leader, and men's coach focused on helping men reclaim discipline, clarity, and purpose in a distracted world.

After building businesses in the United States and competing at a professional level in combat sports, Terry made the decision to move to Costa Rica in search of a more intentional way of living. What began as a change in geography became a spiritual awakening. Removed from the noise and constant validation of achievement, he was confronted with deeper questions about faith, identity, ego, and surrender. Living close to the ocean, training daily, building retreat spaces from the ground up, and guiding men through physical and spiritual work reshaped his understanding of leadership and responsibility.

Terry believes strength is built through discipline, gratitude is the foundation of resilience, and alignment between belief and action is non-negotiable. Through his writing and men's retreats, he challenges men to stop drifting and start leading their lives with conviction.

He lives in Costa Rica with his wife, Lizzy, and their four dogs, where he continues to train, build, and lead.

Scan to Join a Balanced Man Retreat